FAMILIES:
don't you just LOVE them!

To Joan Martin,

a mum to all of us

FAMILIES:
don't you just LOVE them!

Colin Piper

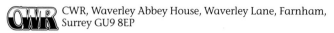 CWR, Waverley Abbey House, Waverley Lane, Farnham,
Surrey GU9 8EP

NATIONAL DISTRIBUTORS

Australia: Christian Marketing Pty Ltd., PO Box 519, Belmont, Victoria 3216
Tel: (052) 413 288

Canada: Christian Marketing Canada Ltd., PO Box 7000, Niagara on the Lake,
Ontario LOS 1JO
Tel: 1-800-325-1297

Malaysia: Salvation Book Centre (M), Sdn. Bhd., 23 Jalan SS2/64, Sea Park,
47300 Petaling Jaya, Selangor
Tel: (3) 7766411

New Zealand: Christian Marketing NZ Ltd., Private Bag 1400, Havelock North
Tel: 0508 535659 (toll free)

Nigeria: FBFM, No 2 Mbu Close, S/W Ikoyi, Lagos
Tel: (01) 611 160

Republic of Ireland: Scripture Union, 40 Talbot Street, Dublin 1
Tel: (01) 8363764

Singapore: Alby Commercial Ent Pte. Ltd., 8 Kaki Bukit Road 2, Ruby
Warehouse Complex, No 04-38, Singapore 1441
Tel: (65) 741 0411

South Africa: Struik Christian Books (Pty Ltd), PO Box 193, Maitland 7405,
Cape Town, South Africa
Tel: (021) 551 5900

USA: CMC Distribution, PO Box 644, Lewiston, New York, 14092-0644
Tel: 1-800-325-1297

Families: Don't You Just Love Them! © **1994 by Colin Piper**

Published 1994 by CWR. Reprinted 1995

Design and typesetting: CWR Design and Production

Printed in Great Britain by Stanley L Hunt Ltd

Model maker: Debbie Smith

Photography: Roger Walker

ISBN 1 85345 073 1

All rights reserved. No part of this publication may be reproduced, stored in a
retrieval system, or transmitted, in any form or by any means, electronic, mechani-
cal, photocopying, recording or otherwise, without the prior permission in writing
of CWR.
Some of the anecdotal illustrations in this book are true to life and are included
with the permission of the persons involved. All other illustrations are composites
of real situations, and any resemblance to people living or dead is coincidental.

Unless otherwise identified, all Scripture quotations in this publication are from
the Holy Bible: New International Version (NIV). Copyright © 1973, 1978, 1984,
International Bible Society.

Contents

Section 4: *Pressure points*

Section 5: *When things go wrong*

Section 6: *And finally ...*

Foreword

FAMILIES: don't you just love them! What a great title! It really sums up what this book is all about because, if you're like us, you'd probably agree that family life is a lot like a certain kind of sauce — sweet and sour!

And that's what Colin Piper captures so arrestingly in this book. He takes the ups and the downs of family life and blends them together without hiding the truth; showing that we're not the only ones not living in perfect families!

Who wants a book that gives all the answers but never outlines the problems? We might be tempted to think that's just the sort of book we'd like, but we soon realise that what is right for someone else may not work for us. That's where this book is so good. It *does* give you positive suggestions on handling family life better, but these suggestions are all set against the background of good, down-to-earth, sweet and sour family situations and so you, like us, will find yourself saying time and again, "Yes, that's just how I feel!"

Just look through these pages — and you'll find things about nagging mums and busy, sometimes unemotional dads; brothers and sisters who seem to get treated better than you; mums and dads that aren't Christians; families that have split up; parents that are church leaders — the list could go on and on. There's not one person who reads this Foreword who doesn't fit into this book somewhere. And, if you go on and read the book, you'll find it very helpful — *we did!*

Rob and Marion White

Thanks

Before you read this book, I think you ought to know that you have a lot of young people to thank for it. About seventy teenagers in total contributed to it, but I'd particularly like to thank Jo Penn and Rob Farrell who helped provide the basic outline; Dave Luck and Jo for all their criticism of everything down to and including the last comma; and Anne Curd for typing it. Thanks also to the mums and dads who helped along the way, including Dudley and Sue Thomas and David and Christine Mitchell and a very special grandmum, Norah Cook.

Introduction

If you're typical:

You'll find it difficult to talk to Mum and Dad about personal things.

You'll find it particularly hard to talk about your faith, even though your parents may be Christians too.

If you're typical:

Little things will bug you about them, like Mum's nagging or the emotional blackmail she uses to get you to do what she wants. Then there's Dad's inability to listen and his embarrassing views, jokes and dress sense.

The biggest arguments in your house will be caused by the stupidest things, like the exercising of *your* right to leave *your* underwear on *your* bedroom floor if *you* want to. And because no one will say sorry, the drama runs and runs. *Coronation Street* eat your heart out!

Life on the whole, though, would be so much easier if it wasn't for your brother or sister, who sometimes seems to get the better deal and most times is generally obnoxious.

If you're typical:

Deep down, even if you rarely say so, you're grateful to your Mum and Dad for all they do for you. And deep down, even if you find it hard to say so, you love them all: Mum, Dad, even that obnoxious, spotty brother. You may not like him, but you guess, if pushed, deep down, yes, you love him.

Of course, your family may have split up and now feel a total mess. You may find it hard to love a dad who doesn't seem to care about you, or a stepdad whose alien family have taken over your home. In fact, though, if you're anything like this, you're not really as untypical these days as you may think you are.

Then again, it may be that your family is perfect. Mum, Dad, even your brother or sister, are sensitive, caring social successes. Your home shines as a beacon of Christian love, hope and faith. Even the family dog knows how to behave in company. Life at home is bliss!

Congratulations if your family *is* perfect! Believe me, you really *aren't* typical and have no need at all for this book. You should take it back to the shop, tell them about your perfect family and claim your money back.

The rest of you may find this book helpful. I hope, first of all, it will give you a chance to see what life is really like in other families, and, through that, help you to understand your own better. Then I hope it will give you some ideas as to how you can make the most of life in your family, making a difference that both you and the rest of your family will be glad of.

About seventy or so Christian young people from Bristol have helped me put this book together. They come from Christian families and non-Christian families, poor families and rich families, large families and small families, loving families and explosive ones, vicar's families, eccentric families, high flying families, incredibly boring families. In fact, they come from most types of families imaginable, but all agree on one point — by and large the hardest place to be a Christian is at home.

This book is based on their stories. It isn't full of facts and figures because we're not trying to prove anything or be clever. But its strength is that it is based on real families. Where necessary, I've changed some incidental facts to conceal identities, but the feelings and situations are real enough. I've also wanted to show you that family problems are nothing new and that the Bible also has a lot to say about the clashes and strains that exist in families. So I have tried to show some well-known Bible stories of family tensions from the inside, through the eyes of the son or daughter in the middle of them. Of course, I can't say for sure he or she really felt, said or did the things I've imagined, but I hope it will help the real story come alive. You'll find the Bible references which are numbered in the text listed out in full at the back of the book. So you can read the stories for yourself, anyway.

As you journey through the book, you'll find some parts more relevant to your situation than others. Do read the other bits as this may help you understand your friends' situations. But when you find things particularly relevant to you, slow down and think hard. To help you, there are regular checkpoints, called "Honesty Tests" which will require particular honesty from you! The idea behind them is to help you think through all you've been reading about, as well as to give some light relief before you dive into another possibly heavy or challenging part. For questionnaire addicts we do provide a sort of scoring system at the back of the book, but the emphasis is very much on the 'sort of'!

If you go through the same emotions reading this book that we all went through writing it, you'll find some of it funny, some of it painful, some of it encouraging and some of it challenging. At the end I hope you'll be better equipped to make the most of your family situation however good or bad it may seem at the moment.

SECTION 1

Do you really want to know about my family?

Families were God's idea, and a good one at that. This section looks at what God had in mind when He put us in families and how you can make the most of yours!

Home sweet home

Liz slammed the door behind her and as she did the row stopped. But only for a moment. "Where's she going?" she heard her step-dad shout. Then it was back to the argument in hand and Liz was forgotten. Such was the story of her life. Her real dad had forgotten her, that's for sure. He'd left her long before she had had a chance to know, let alone forget, him. The nearest thing she had to a dad now was that creep in there.

She was being unfair of course. He wasn't that bad. But she needed someone to take her feelings out on and he did quite nicely, thank you. She'd had enough. Enough of Mum off-loading her feelings onto her. Enough of stepdad putting her down. Enough of seeing his brats spoilt with love and attention before her very eyes. She burned with anger and, not for the first time just recently, felt the tears welling up in her eyes.

She swore out loud and felt better. That was one way to make tears go away. She mustn't cry now, she told herself, as she turned up the path of the house four doors down. She rang the doorbell and swore again.

Stepping into Sarah's house was like landing on another planet. You didn't need to swear here to check your emotions. There was something special about this house. Being a Christian here must be a doddle. She looked at Sarah again and not for the first time felt very jealous, even resentful, of her best friend, and then guilty for doing so. In Sarah's home there was just so much love. There was always someone around to love you, even if it was only one of the flea-ridden cats!

Sarah could talk with her mum, laugh with her dad and gossip with her sister. Even gran was unique in her eccentricity. They could share openly about anything; nothing was taboo. They went out as a family and it was fun. She'd never believed that family outings could be like this until she'd gone along. When she had, it was such a riot. That night she'd stayed with Sarah and Liz was there when Sarah's mum had kissed Sarah goodnight and said, "Love you". It wasn't cringy either. It was real. That was the first time she'd felt really jealous and resentful of her best friend.

She knew she wasn't alone in her feelings. This house had become a safe house for her and her friends. They seemed drawn here, like bees to honey. There was something about it. What was it? It was sort of ...

Liz never had time to finish her thought process. Before she could, she was being hugged and the tears began to flow. There was something odd though about it, and then she realised ... they weren't her tears.

"I'm so glad you've come round," she could hear Sarah telling her, "Mum and me have just had a blazing row."

Jonathan couldn't help it. Up to this point he had restrained one emotion with another. Blinding fury had kept the tears of hurt away. But now as he hugged his friend and felt David's tears drop on his shoulder, it was all too much for him. He found himself sobbing uncontrollably. He couldn't stop, nor did he want to. He had to let his feelings out.

His father, whom he loved, had gone totally beserk. The last encounter he had had with the man he had idolised through his childhood, had almost been the final one. The father he loved had actually tried to kill him. What's more his father had wanted to kill Jonathan's friend, the person he loved more than anyone else. He wanted to kill David.

As Jonathan held David tightly to himself, he gazed over his friend's shoulder. There was nothing on which to focus his sight or thoughts, and both consequently wandered. For a moment his eyes fixed on the rock behind which his friend, up to moments before, had been hiding. Then they surveyed the ground into which he had just fired his arrows as the signal he had really dreaded giving his friend. As for his thoughts ...

What had gone wrong with his family? Could it be that his own father had really tried to kill him? Surely it would have been different if they could have been just an ordinary family instead of royalty? Why couldn't they have been like David's family? Yes, David's family were poorer, shepherds and the like, but they were happy weren't they? They didn't go around throwing spears at each other. Was he to lose both his friend as a runaway, and his father to madness and the growing gulf between them?

Jonathan knew his home would never be the same again. He had tried reasoning with Dad but had got nowhere. Now what was left for him, but to live in fear for the rest of his father's life or his own untimely end. Whichever came first. Oh God, it shouldn't be this way![1]

Far too many young people feel dissatisfied with life in their families. Thankfully, few have been nearly killed by their fathers, as the Bible tells us Jonathan was by his father, King Saul. But few feel as close as they should to Mum or Dad. They look longingly at a friend's home and wish it could be like that for them. "Do you really want to know about my family?", was a question many of them asked me.

Of course, the truth, as Liz found out, is that no family is perfect. All families throughout the ages have had their difficulties. I'll look at some of the causes of these problems later on. But before I tackle some of those specific problems, I want to be positive. I want first of all to inspire you with the concept of family.

Not that many of the young people who worked on this book with me said they came from really good homes. Most, though, had clear thoughts on what a good home would be like, and some ideas on how they could make theirs better. The next two parts show what these were. Even if your experience so far is telling you that the family is bad news — that it can work for others but not for you, certainly not any more — don't give up. Read on and we'll look at the possibilities. Then we'll tackle the problems.

Seven qualities of a good family

1. They care for you

When God made you, He didn't do it for a laugh! He put everything into it because you were meant to be the pinnacle of His creation. Even by His own perfect standards you were extra special. With His earliest look at the first man, Adam, He summed us all up in two words: "Very good."[2]

Convincing proof if ever it were needed that we were made to be appreciated, valued and loved. And not only by God, but by one another, too. This was one of the reasons He placed us in families. Our families were meant to reflect and demonstrate His love for us. So the Bible tells us: "As a mother comforts her child, so will I [God] comfort you."[3] And "God carried you, as a father carries his son."[4]

Deep down we know we need this love from Mum and Dad. A total love like God's which says, "I have loved you with an everlasting love."[5] A confidence-giving love which reassures us about our true value. Strengthened by this love, we have freedom to grow up to become our full selves. Then we can leave the shelter of the family and be ready to become parents ourselves and offer that same security to others.

When this love is weak or absent, we can be tempted to reach out to our friends too soon and too desperately. In our clamour for acceptance we will do practically anything to please. We become what others our age require us to be instead of being what we were meant to be.

But with the secure, committed love of a family, we aren't so scared of rejection by our peers and we can more easily be ourselves. Then we discover that the less desperate we are for friends, the more true ones we seem to attract.

2. They are there for you

Care is expressed by a mum or dad in a number of ways.

They may tell you they love you, like Sarah's mum does every night. They may show it by talking to others about you, like Matt's mum who he says: "is proud of me and is always going on to her friends about me." (Although to be honest I can only take so much of people like Matt's mum.)

They may show you they love you physically (and hopefully sensitively) with hugs or kisses.

Hopefully, they will also show it practically. This means they will take an interest in you and be prepared to give you time. Most young people who told me their mum or dad cared would follow it up when I spoke to them by saying he or she was always there when *they* needed them. In other words, mums or dads made them a priority. They enjoyed their company and wanted to spend time with them. Of course, love is considerate, and if Mum and Dad really care, they won't gatecrash your time and space, nor cramp your style without reason. Mums and dads who are both caring and considerate are fun to spend time with and have a much closer relationship with their children.

3. You can talk with them

Most young people interviewed believed their parents cared for them and would be there if needed. But fewer felt their parents actually made time to talk with them and very few indeed felt able to talk openly with Mum and Dad about their hopes, fears, personal views or feelings. So count yourself fortunate if you can chat easily: unless Bristol young people are more weird than they look, the likelihood is that you, like them, find the art of talking to Mum or Dad is one of life's more deeply hidden secrets. You either wish you could talk more with Mum or Dad, or wish you had the sort of mum or dad whom you could talk to; if you see the difference!

Imagine having someone who you know loves you, who will always listen to you, understand you and be able to cope with what you say. Someone who won't reject you, is trustworthy, won't nag or question you for information, and who is always honest and open with you. Imagine Mum or Dad being like that. However independent you may be, you have to admit that wouldn't be bad, would it? You independent types might still be independent, but this time securely so, and for all the right reasons.

4. They understand you

The more time you have with Mum or Dad the more you are likely to talk. The more you are likely to talk, the more Mum or Dad is likely to understand you. Susan, a girl with wild tendencies, and Steve, who is neither a girl nor has wild tendencies, both told me separately how good it is to have parents who understand them:

"My parents think I'm a riot," Susan smiled, "and I make them laugh. They appreciate me as a person. They take me as I am, an individual, my sense of humour and all the way I am." Steve told me: "I like the way Mum just seems to understand me and respects my opinion."

5. They trust you

The more Mum and Dad understand you, realise what you need, and know what you are capable of, the more confident they can be about trusting you. This means you can be given the freedom and space to grow up and be you. Debbie has parents like this:

"I like the way my parents are trusting. They don't ask too many questions about my actions. For example, they allow Robert into my bedroom. They respect my room because they know I need my space."

6. They protect you

After this, it may come as a surprise to hear that one of the top seven qualities of a good mum or dad was a concern to set restrictions on you, discipline and apply boundaries to your freedom. Then again, you may not be that surprised. As long as they show care, understanding and trust it's good to know someone is watching over you. One fourteen-year-old lad put it this way. "I do appreciate Mum and Dad. They give me freedom within limits. I'm independent but secure."

7. They teach you

We all want heroes whom we can look up to and follow. And I want to suggest that God meant us to have special, close up heroes of our own who were to teach, help and influence us. That's what He intended mums and dads to be. He knew they wouldn't all be multi-talented or giants of their time, but His desire is that there should be enough about their love and character that makes us want to become like them. We were meant to respect not only them but also their opinions and advice so that we should learn from their good experiences and not have to trip up on the same bad ones. This would give us a strong base from which to set out on our own adult lives.

Making it happen

If that's the ideal, what about the reality? It is unlikely that what is written above perfectly describes your relationship with Mum and Dad! Furthermore there may be many reasons for this and only some of them are likely to be your fault. So you may be left wondering where all this leaves you. What on earth you can do about your relationship with Mum and Dad to make it a bit closer to the ideal? The answer is quite a lot.

In fact, the rest of the book is about how you can at least try to have the best relationship possible at home, regardless of how messed up your family might be. Of course if your family doesn't share your desire to make the most of things, this will limit your effectiveness. But you *can* make a difference.

Seven ways you can make a difference

In a moment I want to tell you what the young people from Bristol said might help make those top seven qualities we've been thinking about more real in your family. These ideas are important because you'll find they keep cropping up as we work through all sorts of problems you might face in your family. But first I want to make the most significant statement of the whole book. It might be incredibly corny, but it happens to be embarrassingly true:

THE BEST WAY TO CHANGE YOUR FAMILY IS TO PRAY FOR THEM

Of course, the truth is that when you pray for people to change, the one God normally starts with is you! So if you mean business with your family (and the fact you've got this far suggests you do), first of all pray for them, and then be ready to change. And in order to give you a clue as to what you might be letting yourself in for, here are some ways God may ask *you* to change!

1. Care for them

You probably do care and appreciate Mum and Dad but if you're typical, you may not always show it. Take Kevin for instance. Kev is a lad's lad, a Christian, but not a pudding basin greasy-haired type. Kev is a lad of few words, such as "Mine's a pint, please!" He does, though, appreciate his mum a lot. He told me so. He went on to say he knew she cared for him too, because every day when he got in from work she always asked him how his day had gone. And he liked that! But how does Kev reply to his mum's daily question? When I asked him, Kev didn't have to think long about his answer: "Oh, I say the same thing every day, and that's 'All right s'pose'."

I reckon Kevin's mum thinks he is sick to the back teeth of her repetitive question. She can't know how much Kevin appreciates her interest. She can't know because Kev has never told her! He hasn't told her because, like most young people, Kevin doesn't always think to say thanks and when he does, he feels squirmishly awkward.

Fact: You can make a difference in your family just by learning to express appreciation. You may come from a family where appreciation and love aren't often expressed. In this case you might feel downright awkward in showing it. To make matters worse, your family, initially at least, may find it just as awkward to receive. They may not know how to respond! But believe me, it's so good to receive appreciation, your family will be affected by it in the end!

On the other hand your family may be quite an appreciative one anyway. But, if you're honest, you'll agree that often you've taken their love and care for granted. So again you feel awkward about saying anything now in case it's made into a big deal! You can breathe a sigh of relief! The good news is you don't have to come home all of a sudden showering everyone, including the budgie, with kisses and over the top praises. You can start to show appreciation one step at a time. Young people identified three levels of appreciation which you can build up to gradually.

a. Thanks for someone's actions. This is the easiest way to express appreciation and is a good place to start.

b. Praise for someone's abilities. Like "You're a good cook, Mum". It is harder for you to say but more meaningful for someone to receive.

c. Love for who they are. "I love you" can be the hardest words for anyone to utter meaningfully, but are the three words which draw people closest together when they are said and really meant.

Perhaps the thought of looking your dad meaningfully in the eye and saying "I love you" is not so much hard to imagine as hilarious! Well I'm not suggesting you put this book down now, run downstairs, turn off *Eastenders* and announce your undying love for everyone! They say actions speak louder than words and perhaps it's best to start showing appreciation through our *actions* and then add words to them later.

So we show appreciation for dinner by clearing the table and saying "Thanks Mum, that was great" as we do it. We can use birthdays, Mother's Day and Father's Day to express all kinds of appreciation, not just by writing something extra in a card or buying an unusual present, but also by doing something really wacky. Actually, you don't need to wait till a birthday or anything official for this. In our house recently my two little girls and I celebrated "We Love Mummy Day" just for the heck of it. We put up the Christmas decorations in April, made a sickly cake and planned loads of crazy things. Mum will never forget it, that's for sure. It was a very special way of saying "We love you".

It is a sad thing that telling one another of our love is not at all common in families. Sad because it's important. One lad, Dave, I talked to, was a Christian but would get drunk most weekends. After a while of chatting, it turned out that he liked the experience of being drunk because it allowed him to lose his inhibitions and talk freely about how he really felt. Normally at home no-one talked about the emotions they felt for each other, and although there was love in his home, no-one ever stated it.

If you come from a family like Dave's, however awkward you may feel in giving it, your expression of appreciation may break the dam! It is always easier for someone to express appreciation to you if you have appreciated them first. And even if your home is fairly appreciative, saying and meaning those three words "I love you", can bring people closer than you can imagine.

2. Time for them

When you read in the "seven top qualities of families" about parents being there and spending time with you, that might have filled you with horror. To be honest, you want to get on with your life. Having Mum or Dad around is the last thing you want. As one girl in Bristol said, "My dad needs a brain and character transplant." Taking Mum shopping is not your idea of fun either. You never know what she might do or say and who might be there to see or hear her do it. One lad has never forgiven his mum for going to the hairdressers with him and asking for a "value for money cut!"

But spending some time with Mum or Dad can be a great way of building your relationship. It says, for one thing, "I appreciate you and want to make time for you." For another, it gives you an opportunity to talk. You'll get to know them more and they will get to know you. This is how understanding, appreciation and trust grow, so time spent with them, rather than being restrictive, may actually lead to them giving you more freedom! Also, as you find out more about Mum or Dad, you might grow to understand and respect them more. You may even find such times fun!

Gary and his dad enjoy messing about with cars. He says: "We spend hours driving around and we ask each other questions we wouldn't normally ask. Dad and me get each other into trouble." It isn't surprising perhaps he can go on to say "Dad trusts me".

A lot, though not all, of parents would love to spend more time with you. Effort is needed on both sides, but it might be helpful if you took the initiative. Making sure you are around for a meal time regularly, and being sociable once there, is a start. Seeing any dreaded family outings, however boring, as an investment of time rather than a waste of it, may bear dividends.

Of course there are limits and I'm not suggesting you write off your whole social life so you can watch *Blind Date* every Saturday night with your telly

25

addict parents. But if you give Mum and Dad time and do your best to make sure it is used creatively, not just in front of the telly, then it can make quite a difference to your family.

3. Talking with them

Time together can mean time to talk, and talking is so important to building a better family. Paul spoke for a lot of young people when he complained at how little he and his dad talked together. "We can go for days without talking," he concluded. The first and most superficial level of communication is a mere greeting and, like many others, Paul felt he and his father rarely got beyond this stage.

In this case, the problem was mostly his father's fault. As Paul put it: "It was unfair to expect me at such a young age to take all the initiative with Dad." But his sister was to tell me later that Paul hadn't really made an effort, and I wonder if he had done so, what a difference, however small, that might have made.

Dads can have many faults. A lot are bad communicators and worse listeners. Some refuse to admit they are ever wrong, are opinionated and, as one young person complained, "socially destructive". But not all dads are like this and even if yours is, it doesn't mean he necessarily wants to be. For most it is possible to communicate on a deeper level than "hello" or "goodbye".

The next level of communication beyond a greeting is that of exchanging information or facts. You may be only too well aware of this, because your mum is pushing you onto this level all the time with her non-stop questions. If you have a mum like this, you may be like Karen who deliberately won't tell her mum things because "she wants to know too much". Of course, most nagging comes from worrying, and worrying is a form of caring. However, a lot of mums are for this reason, if no other, lovable but really, really infuriating.

Perhaps one way around this barrage of questions is to go on the attack. Get involved in small talk. Offer some information about yourself. Tell Mum how your day's gone, but then get in first with questions of your own! Take an interest in Mum's day. All right, I know the very idea of this may horrify you! You don't know my mum, you might say. First of all, her life is really boring and secondly once she gets going she won't stop. Actually, that is a very good reason to start! Sure, it may be boring to hear about the price of Marks and Spencer Y Fronts these days, but conversation won't stick there for ever, and when it moves on it will sometimes become surprisingly good.

How much do you really know about Mum and Dad? About what they've done, their experiences as teenagers, their weird dreams, feelings or ideas? Set yourself a challenge to attempt to draw these things out and believe me, your time as a private investigator will probably be very revealing. Let me give you some examples.

One girl who had just broken off her engagement found out that Mum had done the same at seventeen. Another found out that her "respectable dad" had in fact been homeless for a while when her age. Another mum has confessed to having a long-held ambition of writing a book. You would be amazed at what your parents have done, thought or felt. And when you find out, you will certainly understand them and their reactions better; and possibly respect them more, too.

It may be very hard to talk to Mum or Dad. They may find it very hard to be honest with you. They may lack understanding, sensitivity or any degree of social skills. But even if your questions only show you a little of why they might be that way that itself can help draw you closer. If you are prepared to be more honest and open about yourself, and then ask Mum or Dad whether they can understand your feelings or have been through something like this, there's a good chance that they will be open about themselves too.

Paul is right. It is a hard thing to expect the child to take the initiative in building conversation. But he is wrong if he thinks most parents don't want to talk and be honest. Most do, even if they find it hard. Once you start you may not be able to stop; and what's more, you may not want to.

4. Understand them

Better communication normally means less arguments because you understand each other better. We'll come on to arguments later, but at this point it is worth mentioning that conflict can be avoided, or at least limited, if we make an effort to understand the reasons Mum and Dad feel and believe the things they do. The more information about yourself you let Mum and Dad know, the better they should be able to understand you. The more effort you make to find out about them, the more we can logically appreciate their illogicality! Make the effort to step back and understand what's behind what they're saying. It can make a difference.

5. Trust them

As you understand them, you never know, you may find it easier to accept what they are saying and why, when they start worrying. It is easier still, if you have given them a chance to understand you, and trust you in the fullest possible way, too. It is important to give Mum and Dad grounds to trust you. If you prove you will act responsibly you can more reasonably request trust.

Gavin didn't have a good relationship with his parents and complained that his parents didn't trust him. But he went on: "[They] don't trust me because as far as they're concerned I've never shown them I'm trustworthy. They just need to respect the fact that I know what I'm doing." Perhaps the harsh truth is Gavin has made no effort to help his parents understand or respect him. In his case the problem is partly his own.

6. Respect them

The Bible makes it very clear you should respect and obey your parents.[6] This can be very hard and later on I'll look in more depth at some particularly hard situations. At this point it's worth saying that respect doesn't mean you can't question. Respect goes two ways and your parents should be prepared to give reasons for any limitations they place on you.

You may be able to sympathise with Charlotte when she says: "Limits exist up to which I'm free but if I break those limits [my parents] close in. The problem is those limits are fairly obsessive, and so if I am even one minute late in at night I am grounded. Then again they only define the limits when I've broken them, not before. This has really messed me up." Reasonable parents should be prepared to reason.

Of course, it is hard to respect and obey at those times when you do not agree with their reasoning. But it can be important and productive to do so. Some battles just aren't worth fighting. Whereas if you accept your parents' decision on a smaller issue, even though you don't necessarily agree with it, it will demonstrate responsibility and give you a stronger base from which to argue your case on a more important issue later. More on this in Section 4.

7. Learn from them

Sally was one of those girls who looked me in the eye and said: "I want to learn things for myself and make my own mistakes." You may be like her. I think you ought to know that Sally got what she wanted. She slept with her boyfriend and regretted it. She got engaged and needed to break it off painfully. She took drugs and wished she hadn't. Sally told me she will be tougher and more direct with her kids. No wonder the Book of Proverbs tells us: "a wise son heeds his father's instruction".[7]

Every family is different of course and you may feel your family is more different than most! But before you read on I would like you to stop and complete the honesty test on the next page to see how much of what I've said so far could apply to you. I'll say it one more time: I believe these ideas could make a difference. Now admittedly, I am also someone who believes watching Colchester United play football is the nearest thing to heaven on earth, spam fritters are a delicacy and flat caps are stylish. But remember these ideas don't originate with me but with young people whose families are probably as odd as yours!

HONESTY TEST 1

Tick the box at the end of the statement which best describes you.

1. Do your parents:
   a. Show care for you practically by what they do for you? ❏
   b. Show it practically but also physically if you let them? ❏
   c. Tell you specifically that they love you? ❏
   d. Not seem to care at all? ❏

2. Do you:
   a. Appreciate Mum and Dad but if you're honest not show it that often? ❏
   b. Thank them occasionally and do the odd thing around the house without being asked? ❏
   c. Tell them you appreciate them quite frequently? ❏
   d. Not feel that close to them? ❏

3. Do you:
   a. Get on with your own life and try not to get too involved in family things? ❏
   b. Do some things with your family when pushed? ❏
   c. Do quite a lot together? ❏
   d. Share some interests with Mum or Dad and enjoy their company? ❏

4. Do you talk with Mum or Dad about:
   a. Your news? ❏
   b. Ideas or dreams you have? ❏
   c. Things or people you enjoy, love or have found painful? ❏
   d. As little as possible? ❏

5. Does Mum or Dad (choose the one to whom you feel closest):
   a. Listen to your news and opinions? ❏
   b. Tell you a little about him or herself? ❏
   c. Talk openly about themselves? ❏
   d. Make it very difficult to talk about anything? ❏

6. Does Mum or Dad trust you:
   a. Up to a point, but not as much as they could? ❏
   b. As fully as they should? ❏
   c. Not at all? ❏
   d. A little, but they are far too over-protective? ❏

7. Do you respect your parents' judgement?
   a. Yes. ❏
   b. No, because they never give reasons. ❏
   c. Sometimes, but they are erratic! ❏
   d. No, because it is uninformed. ❏

(Turn to page 157 if you want to see how you score.)

Taking the lid off your family

This section looks at your family, member by member:

At Mum: why she might worry and nag, and why she might get over-nosey and emotional. It looks at how you can get closer to her, communicate more with her and help her take a break.

At Dad: why he might find it hard to express emotion, communicate with you and say sorry. It offers some hope of getting closer to Dad whatever he's like.

At mixed up families: how to cope with families which are splitting up, have split up or even, you might feel, would be better split up. It looks at the pluses and minuses of living in a single parent family. It explores how to make something of a relationship with a parent who has left home and a step-parent who has moved into your home.

At brothers and sisters: what everyone feels, whether they are the oldest, youngest, only girl, boy or child or twin.

Pick the parts most relevant to you!

They're only human

The sight stunned him. He had seen people naked before. Of course he had. But somehow this was the most depressing, sickening and bewildering sight he had ever experienced. It wasn't so much the body itself that set off these feelings. Sure, it was past its prime. It was ageing. In fact, it belonged to the oldest man alive. But that wasn't what made it so awful. Somehow, it was a pathetic sight too — not just its nakedness, but its utter helplessness. It was totally intoxicated, drunk. But even that wasn't what made it so horrendous. What made the sight so traumatic was that it was his own father he was looking at. And in the instant of that one glance, a thousand illusions were shattered.

You see, Noah was more than a father to Ham. He was a hero. His dad was, without doubt, the greatest man on earth and very probably the greatest man who had ever lived. That wasn't just Ham's view either. It was the view of the whole family. In fact, of everyone alive: it amounted to the same thing really, since only his family had survived the flood. Dad was the only reason any of them were alive. He was so great, God Himself had chosen him to be spared from the flood. Him only, and his family, of course. So there they were, safe, and all because their father was so perfect.

But he wasn't, was he? Ham looked again at his father's quivering, naked stomach as it came to terms with the unwanted excess of alcohol while trying to maintain breathing as usual, his father oblivious in his slumber of how greatly he had failed. And not only failed himself, but his son, too. Gone for ever were Ham's illusions of greatness, replaced by a new image which would never go away: the pathetic sight of his father's failure.

Ham stood there as if frozen. He didn't know what to do. He never did. He wasn't great like his father and never would be, however much he tried. He wasn't even like his brothers, Shem and Japheth. They always knew what to do. They would react instantaneously in this situation, and for them it would be no big deal. For him it was a shaking, crashing earthquake of emotion. He just stood there staring at the body, revolted, dejected, yet somehow transfixed.

Suddenly, it was as though something inside him snapped and he ran. Out of his father's tent. Just out, anywhere. He didn't have a clue where he was going and didn't care. He ran like a madman. He had to find his brothers. Had to tell them and they would know what to do. In fact, he didn't have to search hard for them. They were just outside. But he had to search very hard indeed for the words to explain what had happened.

Sure enough, when his brothers finally grasped what he was trying to say, they took it in their stride. They knew exactly what to do. They managed to cover up their father's body without seeing the sight which had so upset him, and would do for the rest of his life.

It was always this way, he thought to himself as he sat alone the next day. He messed up and his brothers excelled. He had the hurts and they had the successes. The only difference now was that up to yesterday he had had something or someone to live for. Yesterday those illusions had been shattered. His dad had failed him and it hurt. This morning Noah had woken with the hangover he deserved and in his foul mood had even cursed Ham. But didn't Dad realise his curse meant little any more? It was his failure which hurt the most. Nothing Noah would say again could ever demand the respect it did before. Ham had to face the truth unflinchingly. Dad was just another human failure.[8]

It is often said that when we're children, our parents can't do anything wrong. When we're teenagers, they can't do anything right. And finally, when our hormones have settled down and we get down to life on a rather more even keel, we discover they're all right really! Of course, they don't actually change all that dramatically, but our views and expectations of them do. Parents, after all, are only human, as much as you will be when you become a mum or dad.

Even so, it can still be a shock to the system to find out just how human our parents can be. When Dad cries, lets you down or fails badly at something. When Mum can't cope, when she flies off the handle or gets depressed. Becoming aware of Mum and Dad's weaknesses can be very bewildering indeed, as I imagine Ham discovered. So we need to be realistic in our assessments of mums, dads, brothers, sisters and anyone else who may one way or another make it onto the family tree.

This section aims to help you understand them better and know how to react to them more positively. We'll look at all types of family, and family members, in turn. But first there are some truths that apply to them, because like Noah and the rest of us they all share one thing in common: they're only human! And this explains a lot.

1. They will fail

There will be times when they will snap, go over the top, jump to the wrong conclusions, find it hard to muster enthusiasm for some things, forget, be insensitive, rude, and downright selfish. I'm not excusing it but just explaining it. I know because that's what I can be like, and I know you'll admit you are, (just occasionally!), like it too. Understanding this and making allowances for one another can make a big difference to our relationships.

2. They have been failed

They were young once, and just as you can be easily hurt, the likelihood is they have been hurt, too. Perhaps they come from a broken home, an over-strict, sheltered one, a highly pressurised one or a loveless or unexpressive one. Perhaps they've been hurt by friends, by people they've loved, or by unfulfilled dreams. Basically they may have been hurt by any one of a million things, some of which you are only too aware of because you've been hurt in some of those ways yourself.

This might explain why Dad can't express his feelings or communicate in any depth, or, indeed, why Mum gets so highly strung or depressed. They've carried these hurts into your home. What you may see and get frustrated by is only the outworking of pain hidden underneath.

A number of young people can recognise this and perhaps you can too. But you might be tempted to say, "So what? What can I do about it?" You don't mean to be unkind, just realistic. Well perhaps there are some things you can do. You can certainly pray. You might even be able to talk to your *other* parent about it. He or she may have given up hope trying to deal with the matter. A common response encountered by young people from one parent about the other, was: "I've tried to get him to face up to this for twenty years, but he just won't." However, with some nagging, perhaps this dad may be persuaded to try just one more time to talk with someone about these hurts. Today more than any time in the past we are probably more used to talking about inner hurts and there are more people better equipped to deal with them.

3. They have insecurities

This might be the hardest truth of all for you to accept. "If anyone is insecure around here it is me", is your probable response. But think about it for a moment. Would you say your parents sometimes are out of touch and out of date? Do their opinions and values sometimes at best make you laugh and at worst make you cringe? Do they sometimes really seem to miss the point? Even sometimes fail to understand in the slightest the world you're growing up in?

Well, if you've noticed these things, the chances are your parents have, too. The world has changed so much from the world they grew up in that they may be feeling very unsettled. For instance they might not understand your humour, music, language or clothes, let alone your views. Even your homework might bewilder them. At the end of the day they may look back with longing at your childhood when their influence was still greater than that of the school. They compare the you they knew then to the you they know now. They might not understand you any more because you've taken on board the modern culture they are so unsure about. They may be bewildered by the change. They may even get protective against something they can't understand and are, consequently, suspicious of.

Whether any of this is true of your mum or dad or not, and it won't necessarily be so, there are enough other unsettling things for Mum and Dad to cope with. For instance, there will be little they can take for granted any more. Their job may be insecure. Their marriage may be rocky. Things in their youthful optimism they thought would be unshakeable are proving not to be quite so certain.

Then finally, but by no means least, there is the insecurity of ageing. They may be changing as much as you are physically. But at least in adolescence you have life to look forward to as your body matures. For them menopause marks the beginning of the end, and if their parents, or perhaps friends, have died, the phrase "middle age crisis" no longer sounds so funny!

All this might explain why your dad responds so insecurely in his relationship with you. He might not like his authority questioned and might find it very hard to say sorry. It might also explain why Mum is such a worrier, nagger and a modern-day reincarnation of the Spanish Inquisition! You could have good reason to turn round to them and say "Don't worry, it's just a phase you're going through." But I'm not sure that would be terribly sensitive!

Anyway, I think it is now time I moved on to look more specifically at relating to Mum, Dad, brothers, sisters, stepparents and the rest of the gang. So here goes.

Mums and dads

Richard looked at his mum across the kitchen table and loved her more than ever. His girlfriend, well ex-girlfriend now, had always said his mum was the nearest she'd ever had to having a mum of her own. Mum was like that. She loved mothering. He was so proud of her.

Then he was proud of Dad, too, in his way. He was strong, able and very practical. If only Dad would let him, he could be close to Dad too. Dad wouldn't let him though, and now it turned out he wouldn't let Mum either. Just lately Richard had realised the truth. That whenever it came to decisions or personal thoughts and feelings Dad would shut Mum out as much as him. Which was why, now, more than ever, he looked across the table and loved his mum. They were bonded by the emotional rejection by Dad. Richard had always needed Mum's love to make up for the lack of Dad's. Now for the first time he realised Mum equally needed his, and he was going to make sure she got it. He was useless with words but now he was going to try to say something.

His thoughts drifted on: "Funny how things come to a head, isn't it? Dad has always been closed. He insists on his own way and gets shirty as soon as his authority is questioned. He rarely admits mistakes and never but never talks about the past. All of which is the exact opposite to Mum. How had their marriage survived?" A thought struck Richard as suddenly, and he imagined as painfully, as lightning: "Would their marriage survive much longer? Mum wouldn't leave Dad while any of the children were around. But now he was the last child still at home. In a few months he would be leaving for college. He could soon be returning to a broken home." He dismissed the concept quickly and tried to recall how this thought process had started.

"Oh yes, funny how things came to a head, isn't it? After all this time, what is it that blows everything sky high? The purchase of a new caravan! It seems Dad didn't think to talk about it with Mum and now he's enraged that she doesn't appreciate his generosity. Typical self-centred Dad. He doesn't need to talk things through. He just does them and we should applaud and make excited noises in all the right places." Richard couldn't help himself smiling. It was a bit like one of those family fireworks evening when he was a kid. Mum, his sisters and he would all stand back and Dad would run up and down doing everything. They would make all the right noises then, too, to keep Dad happy. He was so insensitive he never realised they were taking the mickey.

Richard smiled an even bigger smile at the next thought. Mum had threatened that if the old caravan goes, she would too. He could picture her, chained to the caravan and being dragged behind down the road. One thing he knew was that if she did chain herself to the caravan, he'd be there with her. But somehow he had a feeling it wouldn't come to that. He had a hunch that for the first time in living memory Mum was going to win a battle and he would be cheering noisily in all the *wrong* places. At least, as far as Dad was concerned.

"Mum", he stuttered, "I think you're great."

He had a lot to be thankful for. Well, that's what he kept telling himself anyway. His family was so straightforward. He had a mum, a dad and a brother, and, although it wasn't the done thing to talk about, he knew others looked at him with some envy. Their families were so mixed up. The better ones just had loads of kids, the difficult ones had loads of wives and, well, sort of wives, if you can understand that concept. The very worst had loads of everything! His family was great. He had one dad, one mum and one brother. Full stop.

But not everything was so great. True, he had only one mum and dad. And they certainly loved one another. He knew both he and his brother Esau were very much wanted, too. Again not much was said, but you could learn a lot from overhearing the gossip around the wells. Isaac, his dad, it seems had become more and more desperate for a son. But then his granddad's bluntness didn't help. The old man was totally obsessed with this vision of populating the world. And when his son and daughter-in-law produced nothing in twenty years, I guess Mum and Dad felt the

He could picture her, chained to the caravan and being dragged down the road.

pressure. Jacob chuckled as he had before. They must have been totally bowled over when, finally, not one but two sons popped out.

The problem for him was that he never really understood his dad. Mum was great. He felt so close to Mum. But Dad was different. Somehow, Dad was aloof from him. It was almost as though Dad had inherited his grandfather's obsession with the vision for world domination, or whatever it was. He knew it was something special and yes, actually he wanted to be a part of it. But it was as though Dad didn't want him involved. Only Esau. What was it all about?

Jacob flopped back on his cloak and gazed up at the black roof of the tent. Through it little specks of light shone, like stars in the night sky. If only Dad would talk with him. He just wanted to be involved in Dad's life, too.

He frowned at his own self-pity. Really, things weren't that bad. He was so close to Mum. It was almost as though she was trying to make up for Dad's lack of love. Yet in some ways that just made things worse. Again he knew the gossip, even if everyone went quiet when he rounded the corner. He knew he was hardly growing up to become a man's man. Some would call him effeminate. That wasn't fair. But it didn't help that Esau, by contrast, was such a thug. He was all muscle. He even had muscle where his brain should have been. Jacob found it hard to like his brother. They had nothing in common. Worse still, the more Dad seemed to admire Esau the more he felt (and he admitted it was only feelings) that Dad despised him.

The mere fact he was lying here in Mum's tent when he should be out in the fields said it all really. Not for the first time he despised himself. If only Dad would love him like Mum did. He'd do anything for Dad's blessing. One thing he vowed: He would never ever fall into the same trap. When he was a father, he would love all his sons equally.[9]

Most young people agree with both Richard and Jacob that it is much easier to get closer to Mum than Dad. First of all, they say Mum is more available. In other words Dad is often more remote than Mum simply because he is away at work and not around so much. But even when Dad is around he doesn't seem to be able to comfort and care in quite the same way as Mum. Dads seem to find it harder to talk and express affection. What most young people are possibly unaware of is that deep down a lot of dads would love to be free to express their feelings and love and get close to their children. They simply find it too difficult.

Whether your mum and dad are like this or not, you may find some of these other characteristics of mums and dads mentioned by young people ring true to some degree. I'll look first at mums and then dads.

Mum is loveable but ...

"I do love Mum; it's just that we seem to clash so much. Perhaps we're too alike."

Why is it that so many young people end up being driven mad so often by mums they love so much? Well if this is true of you, it might help to remember two things for starters. First if Mum is around so much, it is more likely you will clash with her, just by the law of averages. Secondly if she is around a lot and Dad isn't, she probably feels very responsible for you. Think about it, would you like to be responsible for someone like you?

Who'd be a mum?

Try putting yourself in Mum's shoes. You're probably tired and possibly have other worries on your mind in addition to the concerns of your children. You love your little child and are desperately trying to adjust to the fact he or she is no longer a little child. You are struggling to work out how much trust and responsibility you can give him or her. You aren't an expert, remember. You don't know how these things work. All you know is that he or she is becoming, or perhaps is, taller than you and you feel very unsure of how you could actually control your child if it came to the crunch.

Tales of girls being raped and boys killed in accidents fill the news. The blurred pictures of these young people on the telly or in the paper suddenly look remarkably similar to those of your own children hidden away somewhere. You know you probably over-react because you had a mum like you once, remember. But now you don't quite seem to be able to help it. Most of the time your child is so sensible but just now and then he or she does something ... well, let's be charitable: "something odd".

Now I hope that hasn't put you girls off the thought of being a mum! It isn't all that bad really, I'm told! But it does help explain why most young people I surveyed agreed that Mum was, from time to time at least, a worrier and nagger, pushy and nosey, irrational and inconsistent.

What makes Mum Mum?

Mum possibly feels responsible but inadequate and resorts to worrying. This fuels her need to know and she appears nosey. Then again, if she doesn't feel she knows what is going on or even if she does know but can't fully grasp it, she may make some rather odd decisions to say the least! This is especially true if she is tired or anxious about something else.

Remember there are possibly all sorts of strains on Mum as well, as I mentioned earlier. When it all mounts up, Mum may get weepy and emotional. She may also get obsessive. If your mum's like this she probably works really hard and gets very tired. You might well worry about her but then she manages to infuriate you with her fanaticism about cleaning or something. In the end, instead of expressing concern you end up yelling at her for tidying your bedroom, or else constantly nagging you about it. Then everyone feels bad.

A charter for the appreciation of mums

Now I know your mum isn't perfect. In fact, from all I've written I hope you've begun to understand just how human Mum is. But with some understanding I do believe it's possible to make life easier for Mum. Hopefully, this will also make it easier for her to make life easier for you, if you see what I mean. Anyway, try these three ideas and see how you get on.

1. Appreciate her. You probably do, but it won't necessarily have occurred to you to tell her. Now you needn't get over-dramatic and organise a fanfare every time tea appears on the table. (Though thinking about it, doing that once in a while could be a laugh!) But be sensitive and find creative ways of expressing appreciation. You may be someone who doesn't like hugs whereas Mum is someone who does. Well, pick your moment, summon up the courage and give her a hug, even if it's only a little one! Make her a cup of coffee and say "Thanks" as you give it to her. Just be creative. It may be fun, but more importantly it may also bring you much closer.

2. Encourage her to take a break. If some mums have missed their vocation in life, it could well have been as martyrs. You may be able to imagine your mum going into the arena to be devoured by lions and as she goes you can hear her muttering those immortal words: "I don't know, if I don't go, no-one else will. I have to do everything myself around here. One day I'll go on strike and then everything will fall apart."

Or else imagine the troops gathered in the trenches being lectured by your mum in her floral dressing gown: "I suppose it's going to be me going over the top again. It always is, isn't it? The day you lot lift a finger to help, they'll organise a public holiday." And with that she leaps out of the trench, rolls over the barbed wire and zigs-zags through the gunfire towards enemy lines. You see, that's Mum to the core!

Now it's possibly true that sometimes you are lazy. OK, it's definitely true then! But you may also find it isn't that easy to help Mum, even when you want to. Having fought your way through nagging, emotional blackmail and finally sarcasm like: "If you're washing up, it must be Christmas!", you may find Mum isn't always too keen about being made redundant after all. Her work and role as your carer may have become her life, and if the truth be known, the nagging is as much for her benefit as yours, as it reassures her of her importance and value.

This isn't too healthy an attitude for Mum to get herself into because it wears her down as a person, and makes it harder finally for her when you do leave home. You may already find that Mum hasn't got that many interests apart from you. She may go out to work, but even that may not be a very interesting job. The purpose of the exercise is just to earn extra money so that *you* can be more comfortable.

If this is the case in your family, I would encourage you to start a family conspiracy to free Mum from some of the boring tasks so that she can develop more interests. She may take some pushing. She may feel guilty about going out. She may not even have much idea of what to do. But at the end of the day a mum with interests is an interesting mum.

3. Communicate with her. To avoid the nagging, get in first with as much information as you can tell her. I'm not saying you should tell her everything. She may not understand some things and telling her a bit may be counter-productive. But if she feels she knows a lot and she also feels you're happy to talk to her, there are good chances that she will become more relaxed and less of a nagger. Think about it, there's loads you could tell her which is fairly trivial and won't cause any earth-shaking embarrassments. But it may mean a lot to her to be told these things. It may even lead to the sort of closeness to Mum which seems impossible as it stands.

Dad's just Dad really ...

As we've seen, few young people feel really close to their dads. You may be like them. You love Dad but he's not the sort of person you can talk to or cry upon. It needn't of course be that way as some of you who are reading this will know. Some dads are very communicative. They are fun to be with and play with. They share your interests, ferry you and your friends and support you in your hobbies and school work. They are admired for what they do and who they are and you might be very proud of them. They love you, even if they do find it hard to show it, and will protect you and stand up for you. So dads certainly aren't all bad. In fact, most love their children and wish they could show that love just a little more. They get frustrated with both their general awkwardness and their work which get in the way.

Work as a curse

Don't get me wrong. I'm not saying work is an evil thing. God made Adam to fill the earth, subdue it and to rule over creation. That should have been enough to keep him out of mischief, but unfortunately it wasn't and Adam fell. One of the consequences of Adam's rejection of God was that his workload changed from fulfilment to a real sweat and hard graft.[10] This has had a big impact on families, as many of you will know.

You might have a dad who is away a lot. Then when he gets in, he is often tired, stressed, moody, snappy, unpredictable, preoccupied and remote. In other words, what you do see of him is not exactly a bundle of laughs. When he does relax he is better, but to be honest, by then you might have had enough of him and he might feel awkward with you.

For instance, when he comes home in one of his moods, he might get involved late on in a family argument which he hasn't been around to understand properly. Consequently, he jumps to all the wrong conclusions. He may come in on Mum's side against you, just because that's what he always does. But he has no right to do so. What's more, even when he knows he is wrong, he won't apologise. Or he may try throwing his weight around and insisting things are done a certain way, when if he was around a bit more he would know they are never done that way.

From his perspective he does feel awkward. He feels he ought to be involved but doesn't know how. Perhaps he feels he ought to be in control, which may be why he finds it hard to say sorry. He somehow feels he should have all the answers and should always appear to be right. The sad thing for him is that deep down he knows he is only human and wishes he could be himself with you.

Who'd be a dad?

Now I wouldn't want to put the boys, who are reading this, off being a dad. It needn't be that bad. But it isn't easy. Some times dads spend so little time with their children they simply haven't noticed they are growing up. They don't understand them and become patronising. They don't understand their values and come out with opinions or jokes which appear racist, sexist, tasteless, corny, dated or just plain insensitive. The main points of contact between them and their children then can be those of conflict.

Of course, life isn't necessarily any easier for those not in a demanding job. Dads who are unemployed or else in a dead end job may feel they are letting their families down. They feel failures and can't see how their children can respect them. They may get depressed and end up taking their aggression out on those they love just because they happen to be there. Then they feel guilty.

You see dads have feelings too, even if at times they appear well hidden under skin as thick as a rhino's bottom! Just as you may want a dad you could get close to lean on, respect and learn from, Dad may equally want to be that for you. He may never be the perfect dad. He's only human, remember. But together you might be able to make the best of what you've got. Here are some ideas to get you thinking.

A charter for dads

1. Don't make quick judgements. In other words, don't write Dad off. Make some allowances, too, for his moods. How do you feel when you're stressed out at the end of a really ratty day?

2. Give him a chance. It may take time for Dad to feel comfortable as a dad. You may need to spend time with him chatting. You may need just to spend time with him. Remember he may feel as awkward as you about that. Let him have a role to play in your life. Ask his advice and ask for his views. He may come up with some very odd things, but who knows you may discover there's much more to him than meets the eye.

3. Appreciate him. Try making a list of the things Dad does for you, like holding down a demanding job or even one he doesn't enjoy very much because of his care for the family. Or the times when, instead of putting his feet up, he acts as unpaid taxi driver, homework advisor, or lets you run the video or computer. Make a mental note to say thanks for the things that help you out and that make your life more secure.

4. Pray for him. All dads need praying for. I know. I am one!

You may have read this section so far and thought to yourself, my parents aren't that bad. If that's so, I'm really pleased. Thank God for them and make the most of them. On the other hand you may have read this part and said to yourself my family's worse than that! Well in the next part we look at mixed up families. Then, later on, we'll cover particular issues like parents who won't let their children grow up and are over-protective; parents who seem on the surface not to care, or care more for your brother or sister or their careers than you; and parents who put too much pressure on you! I hope you'll find these sections helpful. But first take some time to think through how much of what I've just written could apply to you. On the opposite page is another honesty test to help you.

HONESTY TEST 2

Tick the box at the end of the statement which best describes your mum and dad.

1. Dad is prepared to admit mistakes and say sorry
  a. All the time. ❏
  b. Sometimes. ❏
  c. Rarely. ❏
  d. Never. ❏

2. Mum
  a. Fusses about things sometimes and worries too much. ❏
  b. Puts silly restrictions on me and can be irrational. ❏
  c. Doesn't trust me at all and won't let me grow up. ❏
  d. Wants to know where I am, etc. but basically trusts me. ❏

3. Dad
  a. Hardly ever says what he feels and only once or twice
     has shown any emotion. ❏
  b. Never says what he feels or shows any emotion. ❏
  c. Often tells us of his love and feelings. ❏
  d. Controls his feelings but will be honest about them
     when he feels something very deeply. ❏

4. Mum
  a. Is very busy leading her own life and sometimes we miss out
     as a result. ❏
  b. Leads a busy life, but still gives us the time we need. ❏
  c. Gives us most of her time but can still get out to do
     some things like work or church things. ❏
  d. Has no interests apart from us. ❏

5. Dad
  a. Understands me, my world, how I feel and what I value. ❏
  b. Tries to understand, but sometimes gets the wrong
     end of the stick. ❏
  c. Hasn't really noticed I've grown up and our relationship
     is awkward. ❏
  d. Makes no effort to understand me. ❏

6. Mum
  a. Will let us get involved around the house if we ask. ❏
  b. Nags us to get involved, but then makes it difficult if we do. ❏
  c. Insists on doing everything herself. ❏
  d. Organises us to do things and lets us do them. ❏

(Turn to page 157 if you want to know how you scored.)

Mixed up families

"Then he said, 'Look, she's your daughter, you sort it out.'"

Up to this point Jenny had been looking me in the eye, but now her head dropped and her eyes focused on the empty coffee cup she was gripping tightly with both hands. The memory of her stepfather's words was obviously painful. Yet Jenny wasn't telling me of a conversation she had overheard the night before. These words were spoken seven years ago. But they'd been echoing around inside her head most days ever since.

Jenny's real dad had left home before she could remember, never to be heard of again. The vacant position in the family was quickly filled by a new dad, though she only ever called him that when caught off guard or in a hurry. He had come as part of a package deal. He would be a dad to Jenny and her younger brother, if Jenny's mum would be a mum to his two boys. It seemed a good deal: three for the price of one. And to the out-side world it looked as though it had worked out very nicely. Who said marriages of convenience didn't work?

Jenny did.

You see, whenever it came to the crunch, the family would always divide right down the middle. He would never be her dad and she would never be his daughter. It needn't have been that way. She had never known another dad, after all, so it wasn't as if he had any competition. But he had made no effort to get close to her and now she didn't want him. Since those words spoken seven years ago, she could never forgive him. She used to hate him, but now couldn't even be bothered to do that. He wasn't worth it. She just ignored him. Seven years ago she had given him the chance to become a dad, but he had blown it, and how!

Jenny was eleven. She had just started her new school. She still felt awkward in her uniform, a little fearful of the male teachers and, to be honest, really scared of some of the boys in her class. She hadn't come up to the school like the others, with loads of friends. She felt, and indeed was, left out. The trouble with being left out is that you quickly become fair game to be picked on and she was. There wasn't anything too wrong with her. At least she didn't think so. She was a little chubby but nowhere near as bad as she had been early on at primary school. But now she was designated for target practice by boys wanting to show how tough they were.

Life became hell. Going to school, coming home, even coming out of the toilets was an ordeal, until one day it got too much. Before she opened the back door, tears were welling up in her eyes. As soon as Mum saw her muddied uniform and grazed knee, and looked up quizzically into her eyes, the floodgates burst. Mum hugged her and cried with her as Jenny stammered her way through a story punctuated with sobs. Then when Jenny had finished, Mum sat her down with a milk shake and a Mars bar and said, "Don't worry, pet. Dad will sort this out."

Doubt immediately swept through Jenny's mind. Dad, she supposed that's what he was, Dad, didn't usually sort things out. But it would be marvellous if just this once he would. Oh, please God, let him do it.

That evening was taken up with TV, tea and homework. Nothing was said. Later Jenny kissed Mum good night, gave Dad a sort of smile and started up the stairs. She stopped after a few steps out of curiosity, and she was right. She could just hear Mum's voice.

"Terry, there's something we need to talk about. It concerns Jenny."

"Oh, what?" He didn't sound too interested. Oh, please God, let him do it!

"She was in tears when she came in tonight. She's being bullied and I think it will be a good idea if you made some enquiries at the school."

"Can't you do it?"

"I just thought ..."

Then he said, "Look, she's your daughter, you sort it out."

Lo-Ruhamah turned away from her father's body. She felt strangely peaceful. She thought she ought to cry, and certainly would when custom required it. But just now she felt remarkably calm, a strength, just like every other she possessed, she felt she owed to her father.

People said she had Gomer's looks. She didn't mind that. Her mother was certainly attractive. All she really cared about though, was that she should have her father's heart. She admired her father more than any man she had ever met and that included her husband. He was nice enough and when she heard her father had arranged for her to marry him, she knew enough about him to be pleased. But he would never win her heart. That belonged to her father.

Lo-Ruhamah's sentiments were generally shared. Hosea was probably the most loving and sensitive man most had met. He hardly fitted the bill as a prophet. His colleague, Amos, who lived down country, was more typical. Lots of shouting and threatening. Hosea could be relied upon to speak of love and not only speak of it, but also show it. His love had saved Lo-Ruhamah from being the mixed up child she ought to have been.

Her name said it all. Lo-Ruhamah meant "Not Loved". Fancy growing up with a name like that! Her younger brother had it even worse: "Not mine" he was named, and everyone knew why! If Hosea was respected by everyone, well most people; then Gomer was generally despised. She was an adulteress of the worst kind.

Poor Lo-Ruhamah had had to double as a mum to her younger brother as much as a sister. She had grown up to all intents and purposes in a single parent family. She never knew quite where her mum was or, worse still, who she was with. The gossip would normally tell her, but it was just too hurtful to listen. She felt ashamed, rejected and hurt, for Dad as much as for herself. How could her mum treat them all like this? How could Dad have her mum back when she treated him like dirt? But that was Dad through and through. He didn't just have her back, he had her back and loved her again. If Lo-Ruhamah could love and trust anyone it was simply because her father had shown her how.

All things considered, she hadn't had a bad life, she thought as she left those paying their last respects to her dead father. She'd come out of it remarkably balanced really. What she had lacked in a mother, her father had more than made up for. Her relationship with him was so special. You know, she may have had only one parent at various times in her life but that one had shown her more love than most children get from two. Really, life hadn't been that bad.[11]

I hope by now you are beginning to realise that family problems are nothing new. The Bible is full of them. It talks of teenagers who come from families just as complicated as yours. Believe me, I've found that pretty reassuring as young people have told me about their totally mixed up families. God does understand and can help.

I know just being told, "Don't worry, God understands," isn't that helpful. That sort of comment is a bit like being told, "You'll get over it and there's plenty more fish in the sea", when the boy- or girlfriend you love chucks you. You just want to hit the jerk who said it. Even though you know it's true, it isn't helpful.

The bad news is, I haven't got too much space in this book to tackle all the problems of being brought up in a broken home. The good news, though, is I have written another book with two friends which specifically tackles these problems. It's called *How To Stay Sane When Your Family's Cracking Up*, and I would recommend you buy it. (But I would, wouldn't I?)

In the meantime, tighten your seat belts, and we will have a rapid trip through mixed-up families of all shapes and sizes.

Family at war — together in pain

Jason told me how pleased he was his family had split up. Life had been hell at home the past few years. Dad was frequently drunk and increasingly abusive. Mum was permanently trying to cover up her bruises and explain them away. It was ridiculous. Jason knew how they'd got there. So did the neighbours on both sides, unless they had not only become mysteriously blind but deaf into the bargain. Jason was so scared towards the end he slept on his brother's bedroom floor.

If your home is like Jason's was before Dad left, can I make one desperate plea: please find someone you can talk to about it. Not only for your sake, but Mum's too, as well as any brothers or sisters you may have. It might be someone at church, a teacher at school or someone somewhere you think you can trust. There are also some confidential phone lines at the end of this book. The people there will also listen and give you advice.

Your family situation of course may not be as bad as that of Jason's, and just because there are arguments it doesn't mean your family is going to break up. Most families argue to some degree (and some young people in the ones that don't, wish they did!). However, if you are anxious and are getting upset, again please talk to someone. I know it's hard. You may not want people to know about your family. You may be scared you'll get yourself or them into trouble. But if you are careful who you choose, it can be a real relief to be able to talk things through.

Family breakdown

Jason is a rarity. For most young people family breakdown is very, very hurtful. When Mum or Dad leaves, it may seem like they're acting out the script of a nightmare you've been dreading for years. Or it may come as a total, out-of-the-blue, shock and leave you stunned. Either way, loads of feelings will churn around inside you.

You may be confused about what has happened. Lacking the full story, you may come to your own conclusions as to the causes of the problems. If you're typical, you'll mistakenly blame yourself when it certainly has nothing to do with you. Another mistake is to secretly blame the wrong person, only to find out the truth later and then feel guilty about your unfair reactions until then. You may, of course, have been too young to know what was going on at the time. Whatever the case is, you do have a right to know what happened as soon as you can understand the truth and shouldn't feel shy about asking.

On top of the sense of confusion, you will also probably feel let down. This is especially true if your mum and dad were both Christians. You may feel more let down by Mum or Dad because of what they believed. Also your family's break up may knock your faith, either because you have relied so strongly on your parents' faith and been let down, or else because you may to some degree or other blame God for it all. Finally, you may find it very awkward with people from church, especially if they find it awkward with you! Once again, my advice is talk to someone. I've talked with a lot of young people from broken homes and all advise the same thing: "You must find someone to talk to."

This may be the last thing you think you can do. You may feel you need to be strong for your mum's sake. But if you don't talk with someone the stress can get too much. One lad told me how he had tried to cope with the stress on his own. The result was his work suffered and he failed his exams. Now he wishes he hadn't tried to handle it all alone. A girl told me she bottles everything up. But now she feels as though the bottle has been shaken up so much that soon the cork will burst. Before she spoke to me, she hadn't spoken to anyone about it and her family had split up two years before.

If you don't tell someone what you're feeling, one of a number of things can happen. Firstly, you may not be able to cope. Then you'll need to take your frustration out on someone and that someone tends to be the first available person. Guess what — often that's the very person you love and want to help. Alternatively, you may try to get out and hide your emotions. Then it seems to everyone you don't care, which isn't true. Thirdly, you may withdraw into yourself, become introverted and shy. These aren't theories. This is what young people say has happened to them.

All this may make it much harder for you to form relationships in the future. For instance, you may already be scared to get close to someone in case either they let you down or you let them down. Behind this is the fear that you'll end up in the same mess as Mum and Dad. The same may apply to your relationship with God. The fact your earthly father may have let you down might make it very hard for you to trust or appreciate God as your heavenly Father.

I'm telling you this not to depress you but to encourage you to talk with someone and preferably with a Christian. I've already said God can make a difference. The book *How To Stay Sane ...* is full of examples of how He has. In fact, the good news is that through the pain you can end up with a more real faith and a deeper love and experience.

Home alone — living with one parent

When Mum or, more commonly, Dad leaves everything changes. Your circumstances change. They may change for the better. There may be fewer arguments. But more likely they will change for the worse with money problems, court cases and the like. Your family is likely to change. Mum may get very low and depressed or she may become much stronger. The same is true of you and your brothers and sisters. Then again your relationships will be different.

One of the good things which can come out of a single parent family is that often the children can become much closer to the parent who remains. Their relationship can sometimes change from a typical mother–child to more of a friend–friend relationship. You need each other and support one another. Life is tough but can be richer, even without money!

It doesn't always work out that way, though. Boys in particular living in a family with a single mum may find things especially hard. You may find your mum relates more easily to your sisters than you because they have more in common. Their closeness can just add to your sense of needing a dad or someone to talk to. You will be fairly bored with my advice by now because it's always the same: you need to pray that God will give you someone somewhere to whom you can turn. For instance: a youth leader, an uncle, an older brother who's left home or a friend's dad.

But it isn't just the boys who can be left out when dad leaves. Mums in crisis will tend to turn to either their oldest child or the one they are closest to. You may be one of the other children, and this can hurt. Often Mum will be unaware of your feelings and you either might want to try talking to her about it or else talk to someone else who might be able to help.

Most young people left with Mum want to be able to help her, and your help will be needed if Mum is under stress. However, some mums try to protect their children from the worry and bear it all themselves which, in the end, is counter-productive to everyone. Others go to the opposite extreme and share too much. If you're in a family like this the burden may just be too great for you. You might not be able to cope with their hurts, depression or moods. Another girl who shared little of her problems before talking to me admitted she had actually got ulcers because of the stress she was under. You won't be able to bear everything on your own, because we weren't designed by God to do so. You will need to share your load.

Together apart — having a dad who lives away

Jason finished telling me his story with a surprising statement: "He's still my dad, you know, nothing will ever change that."

That statement may surprise you as much as it did me. If your dad has caused you and your family a lot of hurt you may not particularly want to know him. You may feel bitter, angry, rejected, or even vengeful. You may want nothing more to do with him. On the other hand, if you have grown up without a dad, then, as Steve put it, "you may not miss what you never had."

Nearly all young people, though, want a dad of some description. Most would like their real dad to be that person, often despite everything he may have done. And the same goes if it is Mum who has walked out. (I'm assuming here it is Dad who has left because from my interviews that was the general rule.)

The encouraging news from the young people I talked with is that God can make a difference. First of all, a number who had prayed had found someone to turn to as some sort of dad. Then again some had prayed and been healed from the hurts they felt. This in turn freed them to write to their real dads and explain how they had felt before: all the bitterness and anger; and how they felt now: that they were prepared to forgive him and wanted him to be like a dad to them again. For some this has marked a new beginning in their relationships with their dads.

But that isn't the end of the story. It really is only the beginning. First of all not all dads replied. One even got his new girlfriend to reply! Some obviously weren't interested in their children any more, and for those whose dads did care, things were still difficult.

Meeting up is hard. There may be distances to travel and time may be hard to find, especially if you want to keep up your social life. When you do meet up, you may feel awkward. Some of those hurts and emotions might even resurface again. There may be other complications like your dad's new family whom you may not like and, equally, who may not like you!

At the end of the day, I don't particularly blame you if you say either it's not worth it or he's not worth it; as long as you don't hide your feelings and do have someone to talk with. If you try burying your hurts, they could well come back to afflict you in later life. In all this the thing to hold onto is the certain fact that our God is bigger than any problem and He can work miracles. So don't give up hope of building some sort of relationship with your separated mum or dad too soon. Be encouraged by Sophie's experience. For years she visited Dad without ever telling him about all the hurts she was carrying inside. Until one day, inspired by her new-found relationship with God as her Father, she wrote Dad a letter telling him how she felt. "It was amazing", she told me later. "When I went to see him next, we just talked for hours. He talked so personally and openly, and cried a lot too. I still can't really believe it happened!"

Stepping into the breach

If you can remember Jenny and Liz's stories, you will be only too aware that having a stepdad appear on the scene can bring with it more hassles than help. It needn't always be that way. Jason's story ended with Mum remarrying and Jason being adopted by his new dad. That arrangement has worked out and Jason now boasts he has two dads! Step-parents in the fairy tales may always be wicked, but in real life, they can be a gift from God!

There are problems, though. For starters you may not help! Liz admitted to me she was being unfair on her stepdad. He wasn't as bad as all that! But she needed to take out her feelings on someone and he did very nicely, thank you. The image of the evil step-parent is not a hard one to conjure up if you put your mind to it.

Often, though, it's easier to conjure these pictures up than it should be. Take Jenny's case, for instance. Her stepdad made no effort to love her and she had every reason to be resentful. Part of the problem is that when someone new is brought into the family or when two families merge, everybody involved tends to come to the new arrangement with a lot of unresolved hurts.

Unless everyone is honest and open about their feelings, it is hardly surprising that these arrangements cause problems. Too often mums or dads remarry without consulting their children. The trouble then is that they don't know where your sensitivities or concerns lie. For them life in the home becomes a bit like walking through an unmarked minefield, and casualties are high.

You will probably feel very cautious about anyone new in the house. They don't know your routine and may try to impose their own. Little habits, like who sits where, then become cherished traditions worth dying for! You are even more wary of someone who is a competitor for your mum's love. Particularly if since Dad left, you have become accustomed to more of it. Finally and most strongly, you may object to someone presuming to take on the role of your father. What right does he have to do that?

If you ask me, you have every right to feel these things. It is your home and your life and you should be given the chance to talk about things before they happen and at any time afterwards. When you do, many of the problems can be ironed out and good relationships can be built. But nothing should be presumed and respect and affection does need to be earned. That is fair enough.

One thing I would add, though, is that you will need to make every effort yourself to accept your step-parent into your home. You may not be like Liz and blame all the world's problems on your stepdad, but are you prepared to accept your stepdad for who he is, without expecting him to change to become like your actual dad? Or any perfect ideal of a dad you might have, come to that? The problem is you may find it very hard to trust any man at the moment, least of all a substitute for one who has recently hurt you very badly.

You will need to talk these things through. If you aren't able to talk about these things within the family, it is important you find someone outside to talk to, who can help you and perhaps even sensitively get involved. This becomes even more important if like Jenny you get a package deal of, not just a new dad, but new brothers and sisters as well.

Little habits, like who sits where, then become cherished traditions worth dying for!

This has been a rapid trip over all kinds of hurtful areas, but I hope the message you are left with is that, despite all the many problems, there is always hope. This isn't a glib answer because many of the young people I spoke to have experienced it. Often that hope has only come through the pain of talking, praying and working things through. But having gone through it, a number have come out the other end as some of the strongest and most together people I've met. Through the pain they have learnt to appreciate what they have, are more sensitive to the hurts of others and know from their own experiences how to help. With God's strength, you can be like this too.

HONESTY TEST 3

Tick the box at the end of the statement which best describes your family.

1. Are you able to talk about your family situation with Mum or Dad?
   a. Yes, we have talked quite a lot or still do. ❏
   b. A little, but there are still things I don't understand. ❏
   c. I've only heard one point of view. ❏
   d. No, because Mum and Dad won't talk to me about it or I don't want to know. ❏

2. Do you feel your family breakdown has affected and hurt you?
   a. A little. It has made me more uncertain about a number of things. ❏
   b. A lot. I still feel the pain quite often. ❏
   c. No. If anything I feel stronger because of all that's happened. ❏
   d. Not really. I sometimes feel a little odd, but normally just get on with life. ❏

3. Do you find it hard to love and forgive one or both parents?
   a. Yes, and I don't particularly want to get close to them. ❏
   b. Yes, and I wish I could get close to them. ❏
   c. No, not really. ❏
   d. Sometimes, but most of the time I just get on with life. ❏

4. Do you see much of the parent who no longer lives with you?
   a. No, but then I don't particularly want to. ❏
   b. No, and it hurts that I don't. ❏
   c. Yes, but it's really awkward when I do. ❏
   d. Yes, and we get on fine and I enjoy seeing him or her. ❏

5. Are you worried that you might make the same mistakes as Mum and Dad?
   a. No, I feel I've learnt from their mistakes. ❏
   b. A little. But I think I'll be OK. ❏
   c. Yes, and it makes me uncertain about marriage. ❏
   d. A lot. I can't ever see myself getting married or trusting someone. ❏

(Turn to page 157 if you want to see how you scored.)

Brothers and sisters

The mealtime conversation was getting crude again. In a while Mum would stand up embarrassed and pretend she had something to do, like clear the dishes. Actually, all she really wanted to do was gain attention and authority and bring an end to the banter which had gone too far. She'd stand up and say, "Really, I think that's enough". She always did, and it always worked.

Mum was great. She'd let conversation run a little wild at mealtimes, but never too far. Just enough to keep three teenage lads amused without going totally over the top. Claire's friends loved it. It was so different from the normal home, having three big brothers competing to see who could get away with the most risky comment. But then just having three big brothers was different enough.

Claire enjoyed it. She'd hate to have a sister. They'd be competing and arguing all the time. As it stood, Claire knew she was spoilt and she loved it. Including Dad, she had, not one, but four men to get her home after parties and things. Then again, she was never going to be bullied. She not only had three brothers but three large brothers. She knew how to handle boys, especially large, stupid ones! She normally got what she wanted, and when she didn't, she resorted to Mum. She would change tactics for Mum. She was no longer the defenceless little sister appealing to male pride. She was now fifty per cent of the female minority and the girls needed to stick together. It always worked. If she was arguing with David, all she had to do was shout a bit louder so Mum could hear and it would all be drawn to a satisfactory conclusion. Well, satisfactory for her anyway.

Of course, there were drawbacks. A male dominated house could be incredibly sexist. She was normally assigned girlie jobs. So while the lads chopped trees, demolished walls or adjusted the TV aerial, Claire washed up, ironed and dusted, like good submissive girlies should! Like heck. Then again sometimes bringing friends home could be embarrassing, especially if for instance your brothers were walking around in their Y Fronts. Home could resemble the Chippendales back-stage. Sometimes, too, she had to admit she felt overprotected.

On the whole, though, she loved them. She loved the way others loved them, too. Home was busy and interesting. There were fights, but it was never boring. In fact, things were livening up again. The conversation was building up to juicy proportions once more. This time she'd be at the forefront. They'd need to learn she wasn't a girlie. Unless, of course, it suited her.

"Why hadn't she been born a boy?" She turned the question over for the millionth time. It wasn't fair. Her brothers got to do all the exciting things, like getting out in the fields and sitting down to those family mealtimes. Meanwhile, she was expected to do all the sort of things expected, even demanded, of females. And being the only daughter there really was no skiving off. Why hadn't she been born a boy?

As she walked past the tent entrance she slowed as she always did, so that she could have a good look at what was going on. All twelve of her brothers sat there looking nothing other than sweetness and light. If only Dad had seen what some of them had been up to earlier, this family meal might not be quite so polite and peaceful. Dinah smiled. Dad probably did know. He was young once. But she sometimes worried that Dad didn't fully understand his large family.

She understood. Being a girl set you apart, and she resented that. She'd love to be in that tent with her brothers. But being the only daughter with twelve brothers also gave her a unique position from which to understand them all. She was spoilt rotten, especially by Simeon and Levi. They were almost fanatical in their protection. And she had to admit she had a soft spot for them, too. They were probably her favourites even if she was fond of all her brothers.

She had to make a special effort with Joseph though, and probably would with Benjamin when he'd grown out of the cutey baby stage. Admittedly, this was partly because of Simeon's and Levi's irritation with Joseph. In her love, it wasn't difficult to pick up their resentment. But then there wasn't much about Joseph to like. He was aloof, superior and brash. Dinah supposed she did feel some sympathy for him. It wasn't really his fault. It's sometimes as hard being the favoured kid as the deprived one. And Joseph was favoured: there was no doubt about that.

Dad wasn't even subtle in showing his affection. If only he knew what damage he was doing to Joseph ... Was he so totally naive as to think his brothers wouldn't get jealous? "I bet he would have hated it if granddad had favoured Uncle Esau in the way he favoured Joseph," she speculated. So he can't blame Simeon, Levi and the rest for resenting Joseph. It's his fault.

And that was why Dinah felt some sympathy for Joseph, even if she didn't particularly like him. He had tried to be one of the lads but they wouldn't have him. So now he acted all high and mighty. "If he carries on like this though," she thought, "soon his brothers will hate him."

Dinah gave baby Benjamin a smile and then a stern look to tell him to sit still at mealtimes. Poor kid. Thinking about it: perhaps it wasn't so bad being a girl.[(12)]

Families are complicated things, aren't they? They always have been and always will be. They come in every shape and size, each unique and so each with its own unique set of problems. I don't know who you think causes most of these problems in your family. Insensitive Dad or infuriating Mum? Or is that particular prize easily deserved by little or big brother, or little or big sister? You might well imagine him or her revelling in winning the "Most Obnoxious Lifeform In The Universe" award and delivering an acceptance speech to acknowledge and thank Mum and Dad for the way they brought him or her up! And quite honestly, you have to agree the spoilt little brat has far too much to thank Mum and Dad for; compared with you that is.

The purpose of this part is to take a look at brothers and sisters in such a way that at the end you will understand them better. Who knows? You may even get on with them better, too. I'm not necessarily implying you don't get on with them; and even if you don't, I know deep down you probably can't help loving them. "I don't like him but I do love him, I suppose," was a common remark made to me by long-suffering big or little brother owners! However, very few young people felt close enough to their brothers or sisters to talk deeply with them, or anything like that. I hope this part will edge you a little in that direction.

I want to introduce you to the Tid family. There's Mum and Dad Tid and then there's four kid Tids. Will is the oldest, closely followed by Mel, then there's Jill and finally the baby of the family, eleven-year-old Blake, who, for some obscure reason (everyone has a different version of this story), is affectionately known as Blo. Finally, there's the dog. I can tell you he's definitely a dog, but

You might well imagine him or her revelling in winning the "Most Obnoxious Lifeform in The Universe" award ...

beyond that the origins of Sir Ray are clouded in mystery. I'll let each tell their own story.

Will Tid

I'm eighteen and have just done my A levels. I did OK, three Bs. (Actually, I think I did brilliantly, but I pretend to be pretty cool about it because, well, it is pretty cool, don't you think?) I enjoy being the oldest. It suits my character. I do everything first. I blaze the trail. I go where no Tid has gone before. I set foot on virgin soil. I ... well, I think you've got the picture.

There are drawbacks, though. For starters, I've always had the rougher deal. Blo has life so much easier. By the way, good name, don't you think? Blo, Blo Tid! Get it? I made it up. Mum and Dad are too moronic to understand. They think we're just being affectionate to the little flabby runt. I think Blo's finally sussed it but it's too late now — the name's stuck! Anyway he's spoilt rotten. Things my parents wouldn't let me do 'til I was fourteen at least, he does at eleven. It's not fair being the oldest. Mum and Dad are strictest with you as they learn their job, and then they ease up with all the rest. Unfair or what!

The problem is, one moment they're being really strict with me, then the next they're telling me to grow up and act my age. I tell them that if they treat me like a fifteen-year-old I'll act like one. You see, I'm supposed to set an example for the rest. I'm supposed to be the live-in baby sitter for them when needed. I'm supposed to fend for myself so Mum and Dad can focus all their attention on little Blo. Well, I wish they'd make up their minds. If I'm old enough to run my own life when they ask me to, I must also be old enough to run my own life when they don't. They can't have it both ways.

Mel Tid

I'm sixteen and unloved. I've thought about taking brown paper bags to parties to help me get some dances. I reckon I stand more chance with one over my head. Then again, if it slips off mid-dance, at least the girl can use it as a sick bag when she sees my acne. You think I'm paranoid, don't you? I know because everyone does. Everyone hates me. Even you. No one here likes me, that's for sure.

They love Will because he was the first. Jill because she's their "little girl" and Blo because he's the baby. Oh, and then there's me. I make up the numbers. You think I'm making it up, don't you? But it's always been that way, ever since I was born. I'm not sure I was even wanted in the first place. Just look at the photo albums. Loads of old prune-faced Will, but hardly any of me. I rest my case.

Good name, by the way don't you think, Blo Tid. Get it? I made that up. You see, I can be clever, if I want to. It's just that I don't always want to. Why should I, when Will's already done everything before me? Even if I do manage to do things as well as Mr Smug, Mum and Dad are hardly likely to get as excited again, are they? And, anyway, I'm not likely to do as well as him. I never do anything as well as him. That's probably why people don't like me.

Don't get me wrong, Will's OK. Well, he is some of the time, anyway. When he's in the mood, he can be good company, and we have a laugh together, mainly at Blo's expense. But it isn't much fun having to follow him.

Jill Tid

I'm the nice, pretty child. You've probably gathered by now that Will is obnoxious, Mel is paranoid and Blo is spoilt. Well you'll be pleased to know I'm balanced. I don't need to compete with Will because I'm a girl and in this male chauvinist environment that disqualifies me from the contest. It's actually quite fun playing the dumb blonde. I have these stupid males wrapped around my little finger. The only one I can't con is Mum but she needs me herself if she is to stay sane with all these guys around.

You certainly learn how to control men in a situation like this. I think half my class live in fear of me and the other half live in fear of my brothers, so life isn't that bad really. I'm a little devious perhaps and sometimes wonder if I'm turning into the character I portray at home. Maybe I'm not as stupid as I pretend to be. The trouble is I'm getting lazy, my parents don't want to push me "unrealistically" and my grades are nothing special. Still, life's to be enjoyed and I intend to make the most of it.

Blo Tid

They think I don't know about my name: I do. They think I don't care about the taunts: I do. It's not much fun being the youngest, you know. I'm only three years younger than Jill, (she gave me this silly name), but it could just as easily be thirty years. I'm the one who's left out.

There are compensations: I am spoilt, I admit it. But even that's not always fun. Going through life as "the baby" or "so and so's little brother" gets right up my nose (even if sometimes it's quite handy for getting into things or getting to know people).

I'm glad Mel is such a jerk, though. Following Will isn't much fun, but if Mel messes up, life will be easier for me whatever I do. What's more, I don't think I'm going to mess up. Mel's not so much a disaster waiting to happen as a disaster expecting to happen. He's a walking education. He has shown me how not to live life! Poor guy.

You know my biggest fear, though. I'm scared that when everyone leaves home I'll be left here all alone. I'll be stuck doing the same old things the other three have had enough of while they're out in the world enjoying life. Then, when it comes to my turn to go, I'll still be Mummy and Daddy's baby, and my going might not be quite so easy.

Sir Ray

If you promise not to laugh, I'll tell you what I am. I'm half St. Bernard and half miniature poodle! Honest! I was a twin, in fact. Well me and my brother actually had some sisters, too, but they didn't last long. Sad really, but that's life, I suppose.

Life with my brother was exhausting. Everything was a competition with each of us wanting to take the lead. But then it was also fun being a twin. There was always someone to play with. Now he's been sold, I guess you'd call me an only child. It has its compensations. I get all the attention and all I need. In fact I admit it, I have become lazy. But there are draw-backs. I get quite lonely sitting on my beanbag all on my own and find I relate better to humans than other dogs these days. Then again, often humans seem to relate better to me than the kids in this family. Can't think why!

Five-point plan

I hope you can't relate too closely with any member of the Tid family, apart, perhaps, from Sir Ray. But these caricatures are not too unreal, as I'm sure you've realised. Read the Tid family's comments again and you may begin to understand what your brothers and sisters might be thinking and why they might react in the ways they do. I have five more pieces of advice for you and, finally in this section, an honesty test.

1. Try to build as close a relationship with your brothers and sisters as possible. Brothers and sisters needn't be there to be endured, teased, competed with or argued with. They can become friends to be loved, laughed with, encouraged by and talked with. You may say quite validly: "You don't know my brother or sister!" But God does. Pray for them and then make an effort. You may be surprised and excited by the relationship which develops.

2. Be yourself. I know it's easier said than done, but you don't need to prove anything. It doesn't matter if you are not as good as big brother. God made you as you, and the most attractive thing about you is that you are you. It isn't that you excel at this or that, although you might. Be yourself, regardless of what others have done before you or what others might do after you. Don't be put off. Give life your all and no one can ask for more. Your parents in particular shouldn't. We'll come on to how to cope if they do in a bit. For now I'd just say, sometimes it may be hard for your parents to understand or relate to you, but that needn't mean they don't love you.

3. Be reasonable. It amazes me how most young people think their parents favour another child for one reason or another and most parents deny it. In fact, the interesting thing was that most older teenagers I interviewed admitted to having thought this way when they were younger. But a few years on, they realised that in most cases the favouritism was more imagined than real. But whether Mum or Dad seem to prefer one of your brothers or sisters or not, you can't impress them by being anything more than yourself. It is very hard if you do feel overlooked, undervalued or misunderstood. But if you do, you are just the sort of person Jesus said He came for. So be encouraged. Pray, be yourself, and when you feel able, try talking to Mum and Dad about it. My guess is you'll find out a lot of the things you thought they thought were more your thoughts than theirs. Think about it!

4. Be sensitive. If you're the sort who can enjoy basking in the glory of your own superhuman achievements, hold on a second. You might be making life very difficult for your brother or sister, without even thinking about it. Now I'm not suggesting you deliberately under-achieve at school to avoid making your brother feel bad! But there are ways of encouraging your brother or sister in what they do as well as ways of being sensitive about how your own successes are portrayed. Don't boast at their expense. Worse still, don't get into the habit of putting them down, however tempting it may be!

5. Be a peacemaker. You may be one of those extraordinary people who have the ability to stir up trouble without even knowing you're doing it! On the other hand, you may know exactly what you're doing. Teasing little sister is a favourite sport among big brothers. Getting big brother into trouble by cleverly stage-managing an argument in earshot of Mum is an exciting challenge for little sisters! So be honest: how good a peacemaker are you?

It may be you feel the Tid family have nothing on your brother or sister when it comes to being obnoxious. But we can't escape the fact Jesus calls us to be peacemakers. What's more, when we do make every effort to love rather than wind up, to be patient rather than be wound up, then dramatic changes can take place. Stephanie, for instance, found that her relationship with Debbie, her sister, changed enormously when she simply took the decision to stop winding her up. Basically, Debbie had nothing to react against any more.

So there you have it. Five pieces of advice to reduce grief and grow friendship with your brothers and sisters, however many you have. Mix these five pieces of advice with prayer and you may find your brothers and sisters are human after all and, in fact, even quite loveable!

HONESTY TEST 4

Tick the box at the end of the statement which best describes your family.

1. Do you or your brothers or sisters
   a. Find it hard and feel like giving up on something because you feel inferior to the others? ❏
   b. Under-achieve and play-act a role which doesn't suit you because you feel inferior to the other? ❏
   c. All find it no problem to be yourselves and do your best? ❏
   d. Find it hard but somehow you all muddle through? ❏

2. Does it appear your parents favour one of you?
   a. Yes. ❏
   b. No. ❏
   c. It used to but doesn't any more. ❏
   d. Sometimes. ❏

3. Do you think your parents *really do* favour one of you?
   a. No. ❏
   b. I used to but don't any more. ❏
   c. Sometimes. ❏
   d. Yes. ❏

4. Do any of you feel regularly left out or picked on?
   a. Used to but don't any more. ❏
   b. Sometimes. ❏
   c. Yes. ❏
   d. No. ❏

5. Is there much competition in your family?
   a. In some things. ❏
   b. In everything. ❏
   c. Never. ❏
   d. Only occasionally when fun goes too far. ❏

6. Is there much stereotyping of character or sexes?
   a. Yes, a lot. ❏
   b. No. ❏
   c. Only a little, normally when fun goes too far. ❏
   d. Sometimes and in some ways. ❏

7. Do you talk honestly and deeply with one of your brothers or sisters?
   a. Yes. ❏
   b. When I need to. ❏
   c. I think I probably could but have never done so. ❏
   d. Never have and never could. ❏

(Turn to page 158 if you want to know how you scored.)

How to live with your family and stay a Christian

This section looks specifically at three different types of home:

1. Growing up in a Christian family. It looks, among other things, at how to find a faith which is real, which you own for yourself and which don't just borrow from Mum and Dad; how to cope with Mum and Dad's expectations of your behaviour, views and faith; the temptation to rebel and the problems of being dragged along to church.

2. Growing up in a church leader's family. It adds to the issues raised in the previous part the further problems of living in the limelight; the lack of privacy in your home; a very busy dad; a critical church; being in the know on confidential information; being used by people as a way of finding out what Dad or Mum think; being tied to a church in which you have no friends, and being made to move around with Dad's job.

3. Growing up in a not-yet Christian family. The problems raised in this part are a little different. For instance: why it's hard to share your faith with your family; coping with patronising, cynical or mocking parents, brothers or sisters; being constantly outargued; worrying about your family's lack of faith; coping with Mum or Dad's opposition, different values or plans for Sunday outings!

Concentrate on the part most relevant to you. But it might also interest you what your friends may have to face!

Growing up in a Christian home

Carol looked at herself again in the mirror. The neckline was definitely too low. She'd have to change it. She wasn't worried what Mum said so much as she didn't want to spend the whole evening self-consciously tugging at her neckline. She wasn't ready to be that daring and probably, she thought to herself, never would be. She was just too unsure of herself.

If you could use one word to describe her life it was "uncertainty". Which was ironic really because she was the one who was supposed to be certain about everything. "On this solid rock I stand". "I can be confident of this that He who began a good work in you will carry it on to completion." She knew all the hymns and Bible verses. She had learnt them in Sunday school, week in week out, since she was knee-high to a grasshopper. But what she couldn't really be sure about was whether He who was to carry on the work in her had actually begun it. Or, come to that, what solid rock she was standing on. She wasn't even sure whether as a Christian she should be going to this night-club anyway. But then was she a Christian? She just wasn't sure.

In a few moments Dave would come to pick her up. Her mum would give her one of those, "I really don't think you ought to be going anywhere dressed like that" looks. Then she'd be off. Life was easier for Dave. His family was messed up and he didn't have a clue about God. But she envied him. She wondered what she would have been like if she'd come from a home like Dave's. She liked to think she'd still be a Christian. You see, she wanted to be a Christian deep down, and probably she was one. Perhaps if she'd had to fight harder herself to be a Christian, it would mean more to her now.

Dave arrived as he promised. Mum looked at her as she had predicted and Carol got into the car. She was actually quite excited. She couldn't help thinking that this is the sort of thing a normal girl does. Dave got in beside her and kissed her on the cheek. As he did, Carol saw the lounge curtains move a little. She felt guilty and embarrassed for a split second but then slightly smug. That'll give Mum something to worry about, she thought.

A combination of the engine noise from the clapped out Escort and Carol's preoccupation with her own thoughts meant she nearly missed Dave's first words to her after the kiss.

She thought it sounded like: "I wish I'd come from a home like yours, you know."

But she just wasn't sure.

James arrived just as the teachers of the law were squeezing through the crowded doorway and he knew he was too late. He had been hurrying, but now he stopped and caught his breath. He wasn't sure why he was doing this. Trying to control his brother had never worked before. He'd never really understood his brother and knew he hadn't a chance of being able to reason with him. Still, out of loyalty he grabbed by the arm a boy who happened to be standing outside the crowded house.

"Go and tell Jesus, His family want him, will you?"

The lad grinned. He didn't need to be offered any payment to carry out this errand. The challenge of getting through a house as full as that would be fun enough. Off he scampered to the door, got down on hands and knees and disappeared between the forest of legs. All James could do now was wait and hope Jesus would see reason and realise the danger He was in.

Oh, Jesus. Deep down James knew his brother wasn't really mad, despite what he'd told the rest of the family just now. Mum knew He wasn't too. It hadn't been easy though, growing up in Jesus' family. That said it all, didn't it? Not Joseph's family: Jesus' family. Odd, wasn't it? But then their family was odd. It was, well, religious.

OK, all families were religious to some degree; and those who had to be, like those wretched teachers of the law, made a big thing of it. His family, though, didn't have to be so religious. They chose to be, and sometimes he'd resented that. He wanted to be normal, to make those rude jokes, swear, tease the girl who lived on the corner. But it was so hard. He wanted to be normal, but knew he'd hurt Mum and Jesus.

Now he didn't want to be misunderstood. Their family was anything but boring. There was so much love. Jesus was also the perfect brother. As a kid he'd worshipped his big brother and wanted nothing more than to be like Him, and still did if the truth be known. But He was a hard act to follow. What's more when he said the family was religious, even that wasn't boring. He couldn't understand it fully, and that was probably the frustrating thing about it. But there was something special between

Mum and his brother. They had some sort of secret. Sometimes he felt jealous about it and wanted to know. At other times he was a little scared of it and was glad he didn't. Silly really. He didn't really know what he thought. Being Jesus' brother and being brought up in His house had been well, different to say the least.[13]

We're going to look at three different types of family. Christian families where one or both of your parents are Christians. Minister's families where your parents are involved in some form of full time Christian work; and finally not-yet Christian families. It would be good for you to read all three parts because this might help you understand the advantages and disadvantages everyone faces rather than just focus on your own problems!

We'll start off, though, in the Christian family. On the surface it would appear a real privilege to have been brought up in a Christian home. The chances are you have come from a loving, caring and secure home and you have been introduced to a faith, a set of values and a perspective which help you live life to the full. You may also have a good social circle of friends, both your age and older.

Of course, life in a Christian home isn't problem-free and things might not have turned out as positively as I've suggested. You may have been dragged to a church where you have no friends. Or had a faith forced on you which you don't want or respect, by people whose love and life doesn't match up to their so called beliefs. Then again, even if you do come from a loving family who hold a real faith and are part of a live church, life, as Carol and many others told me, is not a bed of roses. Let's look at some of the problems.

Tests and trials

1. I find it hard to talk about my faith with my family

For those of you whose families don't share your faith, it may come as a surprise to hear that only a few Christian families talk openly about their faith. They may talk about church activities or that morning's sermon; they may say a prayer together at mealtimes, but that is often the end of the line. Most young people, in turn, find it hard to raise the subject of their faith with their mums or dads. Congratulations if you are different!

There are a whole host of reasons why you may find it hard. Simply because faith isn't talked about makes it embarrassing to start. Not all your family may be Christians and this makes it even more difficult to talk openly. You may have parents with very strict and defined views which you may either find embarrassing or not want to confront and contradict. It may be your faith is presumed to have a greater level and depth than it really has. Then if you talk about it, you may give away the reality of the situation. This brings me neatly on to the next problem.

2. It's been hard finding a faith for myself

Most young people from Christian families seem to drift into faith. It isn't a case of a dramatic conversion from sin, more of a quiet acceptance of what you've always been told and deep down accepted as truth. The problem is that it can be a case of "easy come, easy go". Those who have had to fight harder for faith seem to treasure it more. You haven't fought too greatly for it and as a consequence are more unsure of it.

It is hard having doubts as a child from a Christian family. You may not feel you should have doubts and don't want to worry your parents by revealing them. You might not want to talk about it with Mum and Dad any way because they will only give you the set answers which you might not agree with any more. Nor do you necessarily want to upset them by showing you hold different views on various issues that are very important to them. You may also find it hard to argue with Dad because he has so many more answers than you, even if you question whether they're right or not.

3. I'm tempted to throw it all in and rebel

Young people from Christian homes rebel for all sorts of reasons. Some want to see life! There are advantages and disadvantages about coming from a sheltered home. One of the advantages is that you shouldn't get as hurt as others. The disadvantages include sometimes feeling you don't have a clue what life is like in the real world. This is why a number of young people from Christian homes when given the chance, say when going off to college, "I'd like to spread my wings and live life a bit." You may feel like that.

Alternatively you may, like Carol, question the reality of your faith and may, be finding it difficult to get answers to your questions. If that's so, you probably won't be that happy in your faith. You may be questioning whether it really is for you and you then start looking for where the real "you" can fit in and be happy. If at this point a non-Christian boy or girlfriend comes along and does offer what seems to be real love and happiness, then you may be tempted to chuck your faith in. You probably won't chuck it in completely, but then you might never have been into it completely either.

Finally and most sadly of all, you might have been put off faith by what you've seen or experienced in your home. Your parents may be over-strict, hypocritical or just plain embarrassing. It may be your church that is the problem: perhaps it's all crushingly familiar and boring, or maybe you see double standards there. Either your family or church might have expectations of you that you should behave, dress or achieve in a certain defined way. This may have nothing to do with what the Bible says; it's just your parents' or the church's "house rules" which dictates that you shall not shave part of your hair and you shall stay on to take A Levels. You may be left wondering if your academic success and general acceptability in the adult world is more important to everyone than your happiness and the reality of your faith.

4. I'm fed up with being dragged along to church

Most children of Christian families are taken to church whether they like it or not. Most teenagers are given the choice. The ones who choose to go normally do so because they have friends there. They go for the social side more than anything else. Well, they do at first anyway.

Those who choose not to go do so because it is boring or they have no friends there. There may be young people at church but these might not be the ones they can easily relate to.

Of course, some go just because they want to and they enjoy it, a few because they are made to, and finally some, not because they want to or are made to directly, but because they just don't want to hurt Mum and Dad and, anyway, have got into the habit of going. In this last group there are some who wished they could change churches and go to a more lively church where their friends go but feel they will disrupt things or let the family down if they do.

Now you probably knew all this, either from your own experience or that of your friends. What you want are some answers.

Well, I can't promise you the instant antidote to every problem, but here are seven ideas which might help.

Seven steps to surviving in a Christian home

1. Remember the positives

I hope that a lot of young people from Christian homes who have read the first half of this chapter will be able to say "That isn't true of me." Life is never problem-free, but coming from a Christian home needn't and shouldn't be one big problem. There should be plenty of benefits. Sometimes, though, it is hard to see the benefits when we don't want to. This is why, however you feel about Mum and Dad, it is a good exercise to stop and think about the positives before you do anything else. Why not write them down?

2. Challenge the reality of your faith

It is no bad thing for anyone to reassess what their own hope and faith is based on. In fact, I believe it is particularly important you do so at some stage, if you come from a Christian home. Have you ever come to the point in time or period in time when you have decided Jesus really was for you? Have you ever sat down honestly and worked out what your priorities in life are? Are you for instance living for yourself or living for God? It is all too easy to avoid making these assessments and instead just make assumptions.

I would recommend you take a totally fresh look at everything. This is a good exercise for everyone from time to time. Pray and ask God to show Himself to you. Read the Bible, especially the Gospels, as though it were a book you'd never picked up before. Read books about Christians, some from Christian homes, some who weren't. Go back to basics and challenge yourself with a fresh look at everything.

3. Ask questions

If you are going back to basics it may be a good idea to tell some people what you are doing. This will then free you to ask the questions you want to. My guess is most people will be pleased to hear what you are doing and encourage you in it, that is as long as you present it as a positive exercise. That goes for your family, too. Who knows, it may get your family talking. It may even get them reassessing traditions and ways which aren't so much an expression of their faith, but just habits which have evolved over the years. Your fresh look may encourage the rest of the family into a fresh look at a lot of things.

There's no reason why you shouldn't include in this exercise your brothers and sisters who might not be Christians. If they think you are honestly trying to sort out your own thinking and not change theirs, they will probably be more inclined to answer — and think things through for themselves!

4. Try other churches

This may be a good time to broaden your own experience a bit and try other churches to see how they worship. Believe me, it's quite fun going along to a friend's church. You may be able to persuade your youth leader to take all of you along on a visit to another church and their youth group. You may even find your own church wasn't as bad as you might have thought. On the other hand, you might find another church in which you find it easier to grow as a Christian.

Changing churches may cause some concern at home. You might need to come to some compromise arrangement and definitely will need to explain carefully why you want a change. At the end of the day, the reality of your faith is more important than which church you attend. Your parents ought to agree with that, even if they'd prefer you to stay at their church. You may find, on the other hand, that they use you as an excuse to change churches themselves. I promise you one thing: as soon as you start asking questions and talking about things, other members of your family will start talking about things they've been putting off thinking about.

5. Talk to your school friends

Again you may like to tell some of your non-Christian friends something of what you are doing. Ask them what they are basing their life on, what they enjoy about life and what they fear. As with brothers and sisters, if they don't feel got at themselves, they will probably be more inclined to answer and think things through.

Be warned though: you will probably find a lot of your friends have given very little thought about what their ideas or actions would lead to. This should make you cautious about some of their answers. For instance, some may say, sex is good and exciting. Well, if you think about it, the answer is yes, sex is good and exciting, but that doesn't necessarily mean sleeping around is the *best* way to live. The *best* way, in my book (and more importantly in God's) is to save it for marriage. And too many lose the *best* in taking what seems good at the time, without thinking things through enough first. You'll probably find the lives of some of your friends which look so exciting from a distance are not at all exciting when you get talking about them. Which is why I recommend you talk to them!

6. Talk with Mum and Dad and others about yourself

You shouldn't be made to fit a mould, whether created by your family or yourself. Do try talking about your feelings, ambitions and fears. Try telling Mum and Dad if you find some expectation restrictive or intimidating. As long as you approach the discussion positively, my guess is that most parents will appreciate the opportunity to chat. Then again they may not be aware of expectations they have created unintentionally until you talk about them.

And now a Family Health Warning: remember in all this that your attitude and manner is as important as what you say. If you come across as critical and rebellious, Mum and Dad will go on the defensive. But if you show you want to grow and mature and come across as thoughtful and appreciative, Mum and Dad are much more likely to be open to listen.

7. Make a stand in your own right

This is the most significant thing you can do to make your faith real, whether you come from a Christian family or not. All of us have the chance to prove our faith if we want to. We can get involved in some form of outreach or expedition. At times like these, whatever background or family we come from becomes irrelevant. The only thing that counts is how real our faith is. If it wasn't before, it will be by the end.

At the end of the day, you may still get embarrassed by your parents' odd views. There may still be unwelcome expectations placed on you. Your family may still find it awkward to talk about Jesus or pray. But at least you yourself could have a faith that is real enough to cope with all these things.

HONESTY TEST 5

Tick the box at the end of the statement which best describes you.

1. Are you glad you come from a Christian family?
   a. Yes. ❑
   b. Most of the time. ❑
   c. In some ways. ❑
   d. No. ❑

2. Have you found it hard to come to a real faith of your own?
   a. A little, but I now know what I believe. ❑
   b. Very hard and I still am uncertain how real my faith is. ❑
   c. I am not a Christian. ❑
   d. No. Coming from a Christian family only helped me. ❑

3. How do you respond to what your parents believe and the way they live?
   a. I'm a Christian but I don't agree with a lot of their views or ways or their strictness. ❑
   b. I've rejected all they stand for. ❑
   c. I admire them and their faith very highly. ❑
   d. I admire them but don't agree with a few of their views. ❑

4. How easy do you find it to talk about your faith at home with Mum or Dad?
   a. We never talk about anything to do with faith. ❑
   b. We talk quite openly and personally. ❑
   c. We could talk if we wanted to but don't often do so. ❑
   d. We only talk about activities, never personal faith. ❑

5. Do you feel under pressure to behave in a certain way because you come from a Christian home?
   a. I'm allowed to be myself. ❑
   b. I'm told I can be myself but I still feel under some pressure to be and do certain things. ❑
   c. I feel under a lot of pressure and struggle with it. ❑
   d. I have deliberately reacted against it. ❑

(Turn to page 158 if you want to see how you scored.)

Growing up in a minister's home

They were an unusual mixture. Each looked, spoke, even laughed differently. None had met before. Yet they sat there as though they had everything in common and had known each other for years. You see, there was one thing which bound these girls together. One thing which meant that over the next forty-five minutes they would be able to look each other in the eye and say with some excitement, "Yes, I do understand". Each was a church minister's daughter.

I'd interviewed sons and daughters of full-time Christian workers of various shapes and sizes, but this little group was the most memorable. Although they were all girls with dads in full-time church leadership, they echoed themes common to both sons and daughters with mums, as well as dads, in leadership positions.

I knew as soon as we arranged our chairs into a circle that it was going to be a very significant time. The young people obviously felt it too. Each had a sense of expectation, even apprehension, that the others might understand the hurts and hassles she had had to bear alone for so long. It was to prove a very emotional time.

The seven of us were sitting in a corner of a large, emptying hall after a Christian meeting. We didn't have long so I thought we ought to get straight to the point. I took a deep breath and asked: "So what's so hard about being a minister's daughter then?"

Acting a part

"You can't be you, that's what. You're expected to behave in a certain way." Cathy was the first to answer and all looked at her, nodding, agreeing, almost cheering. "Yes," they were saying, "That's what's so hard." And from that moment on I lost track of who said what. I sat desperately trying to keep up with my notes as the group began to pour out feelings locked away for so long.

One girl complained that everybody was always watching her. She couldn't put a foot wrong. Another added she was expected to be at all the church functions and worse still, always be happy. "Yes," said another, "And wear a skirt and look respectable." Another joked that one day she'd like to dye her hair green, spike it and walk into church. That would reduce the average age of the congregation. It was so easy to shock and so tempting, but she couldn't: she knew it would land Dad in it.

I think it was Cathy, but I can't be sure, who took up the conversation again at this point as she told her story. She had fallen in love with a non-Christian boyfriend and no one seemed to understand. She was confused. She didn't know what she thought and couldn't talk to anyone. As tears welled up in her eyes, she concluded: "Everyone assumes you believe and are all sorted out. You can't ask questions. You can't have doubts. You're the vicar's daughter. You must be a Christian. You always have been."

Once again, everyone agreed. Some felt that by admitting doubts to people in the church they'd be letting Dad down. What was sadder still was that few felt they could express their doubts and confusion even at home. Someone said her parents lived in another world. Another felt hers had been time-warped from some century long before. Most felt they didn't know their parents well enough to talk to.

The invisible man

"Dad works so hard, we never see him." The house was always full of people. No-one could go home and relax. Their homes weren't normal. They didn't know what they were walking into. Odd people would turn up on the doorstep. One girl would sit down in the lounge to watch *Neighbours* and be kicked out for a meeting. Meetings, meetings, every night meetings. Home is never your own. Even walking down the stairs to the kitchen in your dressing gown could be like going down the cat-walk at the Paris Fashion Show. Just when you most want your privacy you meet the men's club in the hall on their way out.

Dad spends so much time sorting out everyone else's problems he has no time for his own. But then vicars don't have problems, do they? Their families are perfect.

Let's pretend

"We're expected to be the perfect model family." But it's a sham. One girl, Marion, told of a period she went through when she resented it all so much she ended up almost hating Mum. She had to go to church "for appearances". So when a lady came up to her, smiled, and said; "It's so lovely to see how you all get on so well as a family," she wanted to scream. Only she couldn't, of course: "for appearances".

"Even friends can put you in a box and make you play a role. You just can't be yourself. Whatever that is." Everyone knew what it was like to be left out because you're the vicar's daughter. Friends don't invite you to things because they don't think you can have fun. You want to shout out that you can have fun. That you're normal. You're not so holy that everything you do must be holy. You almost want to shock them. You can smoke. You can drink. To say, "Look, see". But then when you do, you find out they're right. If something happens, and you're there, it will get back to your parents and be around the church in no time. No-one else may get the blame, but you will. Your friends are right: you are a liability.

Boys aren't keen on going out with you. If they do, the gossip goes around the church. "Really my life isn't that interesting. One day I'll do something which will interest them, all right!" was one exasperated comment. It can be very lonely being a minister's child. It can also be tough. Kids at school don't understand. "They joke my dad must be a monk and I'm a vestal virgin." You become a freak, an outsider, a novelty piece. One girl cried when a picture of her family appeared in the paper under the heading of "New Vicar Comes To Town". There she was looking wonderfully angelic all those years ago. She didn't know about the photo until the boys in her class showed it to her and laughed. It was her welcome to her new school. Oh and that's another thing ...

On the move

"You can keep moving house, so just when you do get settled and make friends you leave them all behind and have to start all over again." Someone complained that she only knew a move was possible when Mum told her that Dad had been to some interviews. It was OK when you were younger. It was an adventure then, but not when you are fifteen. To make matters worse, you never knew what sort of church you were going to.

"You have to go to church. More than that, if you're the vicar's daughter, you should be involved." Sometimes you don't want to go to everything. Others have a choice. They needn't go to the youth meeting if there is a party on that night. More to the point, they can change churches if all the young people go to the one down the road with the lively youth group. You can't. You may be the youth group, but you have to stay so that you can be there for those four thirteen-year-old boys ready to come up next year.

It wasn't all doom and gloom. Some of the girls had close friends. Some were treated as ordinary human beings at school and so didn't need to go over the top to prove they weren't some alien species dropped to earth with the last meteor shower. But even then it was often hard, to know who were real friends and who you could trust.

Information please

"People keep sucking up to you and want to impress you. They want information out of you and want to know what your Dad thinks about things." It seems it isn't so much a spirit of love which binds some churches together as a spirit of noseyness. It is easy to get cynical. You see hypocrisy, manipulation, politics and backbiting first-hand. You hear about Jesus secondhand. It would be all right but ...

"You are privy to information talked about at home you know is confidential. Dad says "This mustn't go beyond this house". But it isn't as easy as that. You know about everyone's lives". One girl moaned that she felt like her Dad's private secretary, and this presents another problem. Most stresspoints seemed to come because no-one wanted to let Dad down. You see, despite everything, Dad is Dad and you love him. This makes life very hard, especially when ...

Taking "stick"

"You hear people criticise him for what he says or does." You know how hard Dad's worked and when people take him for granted or, worse, take him apart, anger, bitterness, all sorts of feelings well up inside. He's criticised for his work, for what he spends his money on (what there is of it), and worst of all, for the way he's brought you up. You don't know why he bothers. The whole family feels the criticism and it can throw a cloud over any time you do have together.

Is it any wonder ministers' children can go off the rails? It is so easy to shock the "inside" world of the church, and sometimes it's the only way of being accepted by your friends on the "outside". It is so hard to find a real faith for yourself and sometimes its so easy to be put off by the hypocrisy of others. But most of the ministers' sons and daughters I've met have stayed on the rails. Some only just and others have gone off and come back on. But it's possible! Here are their tested ideas on how to survive as a minister's son or daughter.

Eight ideas for surviving in a minister's family

1. Remember the positives

If you've read the advice given in the part on growing up in a Christian family you'll find some of the advice here similar. But that's not surprising really. After all, you are a Christian family of a very specific kind.

It is easy to dwell on the negatives when you get into a negative frame of mind. I hope being a minister's son or daughter isn't all negative, though. Some of you have the opportunity to meet people from all over the world and that can be interesting. There must be some folk who come around you're glad to see. Having Dad around during the day might be a bonus. Perhaps you have a nice house and garden. Think about it. Even write down the positives against the negatives. Be balanced.

2. Talk about the problems

Other people book Mum or Dad's time, so why shouldn't you? Tell them you want to talk about some of the ways you feel. It may help to write them down, even in a letter, and then work through them. Cover the positives first and then the negatives. The thought may sound ridiculous to you. It may scare you. You may think they will never understand. But you need to summon up the courage and give it a try.

Normally Mum and Dad will do their uttermost to understand, because normally they love you. They may have trouble expressing love and care. They may find it as hard to talk to you as you do to them. But when you try, you may be surprised at how positive the outcome is. One word of warning: your attitude is very important. It needs to be balanced, reasonable and honest!

3. Ask for time

Dad is head of your family before he's head of the church family. Mum is first and foremost your mum, even though she may sometimes appear to be like a mum to everyone else as well. They almost certainly know that: it's just very easy to get so preoccupied with something that you lose all track of time and perspective. This is why it's so important to talk about your feelings. You will probably find you agree on a lot of things! So you might want to ask for more time. Time to do things together so you can chat and understand each other better. Get out if necessary. Go for an "Early Bird, Two For The Price Of One" pizza. Educate Dad. Take him to see one of those awful American comedy films. It could be a laugh. What's more it will probably do him a lot of good as well.

4. Ask for privacy

You need a home, and if home never feels like it, tell Mum and Dad. Ask for one evening when all meetings happen elsewhere. Then you can curl up in your favourite armchair in your favourite night-shirt, have choc ice and chips and watch the millionth rerun of *Grease* on the telly, and know that no-one is going to burst in and be offended by the sight of your knee caps.

5. Ask for space

This is harder but, it may be very important to you. You may need to step out of the public eye for a bit. You have enough hassles growing up without taking on extra ones. It would be great if Dad was prepared to take the initiative in suggesting this break. Perhaps you might suggest that he suggests it! Then he can say to everyone he was concerned that it wasn't healthy for you only ever to be involved in things he was at least ultimately responsible for.

Therefore, he's suggested you don't go to the youth group every week for a bit but that you go out with friends, perhaps to a different church youth group. What's more, you don't have to be at all church activities. With the ones you do go to, you are there, not because you are the vicar's daughter, but in your own right like any ordinary young person. You are there because you want to be and choose to be.

6. Be yourself

You may need to explain to Mum and Dad your feelings, about the pressures and expectations you sense, and be honest with them about your doubts, questions and the state of your faith. I gave in the previous part of this section some ideas of how you might be able to sort out what you believe and what your priorities are. You may like to go back and look at them again and think through which of those you could apply in order to help you sort out the questions you have.

The chances are, Mum and Dad aren't really aware of the pressures you're under. The probability is that they will care and do their best to understand and help remove them. The way to start sorting these things out is to talk.

7. Ask for sensitivity

This might be from Mum and Dad. You may need to ask them not to talk about things in front of you if you find it a burden. It may be from others. You may have to ask them politely not to ask you questions or not to say hurtful things about your Dad or Mum in front of you. Unfortunately, most people just don't think and need to be told.

8. Ask for stability

You ought to know if your life is going to be disrupted in any way. It is your life. So if a move is imminent, you should at least know and be in on the decision-making. In fact, I think it could be reasonable for you to have the opportunity to veto a move. Talk to Mum and Dad about this, but do so reasonably, and hopefully Mum and Dad will be reasonable with you too.

I don't know how many of these ideas are relevant to you, but I do know it is possible more than to survive in a minister's home, but rather to thrive. This honesty test might help you think through your views of home.

HONESTY TEST 6

Tick the box at the end of the statement which best describes you.

1. Are you glad you come from a minister's family?
   a. Yes. ❏
   b. Mostly. ❏
   c. In some ways. ❏
   d. No. ❏

2. Do you feel the work deprives you of Dad's or Mum's time?
   a. Occasionally. ❏
   b. A lot of the time. ❏
   c. Totally. ❏
   d. Not really. ❏

3. Do you feel you're living under a spotlight and resent being expected to behave in a certain way?
   a. Yes and it bothers me a lot. ❏
   b. Yes and it's turned me right off Christianity. ❏
   c. Not really. ❏
   d. Sometimes, but I'm able to cope. ❏

4. Do you have questions you'd like to ask but are either embarrassed to raise them or have no one to talk to?
   a. Yes: loads. ❏
   b. Not really. ❏
   c. I've some questions but I'm able to work them through. ❏
   d. I've some questions and am struggling with them. ❏

5. Do you get distressed by what people say to you about Dad or Mum and the church?
   a. Not really. ❏
   b. Occasionally, but most of it is OK. ❏
   c. Quite a lot and it hurts. ❏
   d. I couldn't care less about the church or what people say. ❏

6. Do you enjoy going to your father's or mother's church?
   a. Most of the time. ❏
   b. Not really. I just feel I have to. ❏
   c. I don't go to any church. ❏
   d. I enjoy going; or Mum and Dad let me go to my own church. ❏

(Turn to page 158 if you want to see how you scored.)

Growing up in a not-yet Christian home

Phil sat down on the edge of his bed. It was dark but he didn't feel like turning the light on. He just sat there, the light reflecting his mood. He was unable to summon up the enthusiasm to do anything. He was fed up and, if he was honest, he'd have to admit he was quite enjoying it. That might be odd, but you ended up being odd when you lived in a family like this. It got to you in the end. Coming through the back door sometimes was a bit like it must have been for Alice to go through the looking glass. Take this evening for instance ...

Phil was high on his way home from school. He was intoxicated with the success of his school Christian Union. Ten people had come. They'd hit double figures for the first time in weeks and they'd had a brilliant debate about the Christian view of sex. To be honest, the fluorescent pink posters with SEX written in massive bold print across the middle might have influenced Phil's four friends to come. But that was beside the point. They were *his* friends and they'd come to *his* Christian Union. He had led it and it had gone well. He was a success.

Suddenly a bit of realism and honesty brought him back down to earth. No-one had actually become a Christian. In fact, none of his friends had actually said anything. But then success is relative, he reasoned. And that's the problem. "Success is relative, and I've had no success with mine — relatives that is." (Phil dreamt one day of being an evangelist and prided himself on how clever he was with words.) He would put that right tonight. He was on a good run today and perhaps, just perhaps, Mum would listen.

She didn't. He walked through the door ready to be asked how the day had gone and ready to tell Mum about the CU (carefully missing out any reference to sex). Instead, he got a monologue he'd heard many times before about how late in he was the night before, what a mess his bedroom was in and how he treated the place like a hotel. It ended as usual with those fateful words: "Philip," (Why could she never call him Phil like everyone else does?) "If you call yourself a Christian, it's time you started acting like one."

He should have realised that this was neither the time nor the place to share the marvellous news of God becoming man and dying for our sins. But either he was just too high or, more likely, that all-too familiar comment about calling himself a Christian had riled him. So off he set. His words tumbled out more like a racing commentator wanting the loo than the cool evangelist he could see himself becoming. His faith did mean something to him, and it didn't matter what persecution Mum or anyone else gave him, it was real. He'd seen the evidence today. Loads of people had come to the CU. It had been brilliant. He'd given a fantastic talk on sex and …

Sex. He'd said it. He'd said sex to his mum. He nearly died. Perhaps she hadn't noticed. She smiled. She had noticed. She loved to tease him about sex. She always said, "My mum teased me. Now it's my turn to do it to you."

What followed was a second monologue. Mum started by poking fun at the adolescent's fascination with all things sexual and then moved on to Phil's general gullibility about life, the universe and everything … but mainly God.

Halfway through Mum's piece, Dad came in, grunted something unintelligible as he always did (Phil had never understood the greeting, but then Dad and he rarely spoke the same language) and disappeared into the lounge to wire himself up to the telly. That was his family. Mum: more opinions than braincells, always right while everyone else is always wrong. Dad: no opinions, no comment, probably no braincells. Jenny (Jennifer to Mum): like Dad. Debbie (Deborah to Mum): like Mum, poor kid.

Phil lay back on his bed and hit the CD, deliberately knocking the brass knob *en route*. His room shook to the apt refrain of "Knock, knock, knocking on heaven's door." Until, that was, Mum marched in, turned it down to Radio Two levels and marched out muttering: "If you call yourself a Christian, it's time you started acting like one."

"It'll be all right son. You'll live. Go and put it in some water. Go on, and be more careful next time."

Joseph half patted his son on the back and half pushed him on his way. Jesus fought back the tears and ran outside to find the water container. He thrust His hand in, felt the instant relief, lent back against the wall and sighed. Dad was great. He loved him. He was such a good teacher and so patient.

Jesus lifted His thumb out of the water, saw the throbbing bruise, and doubted if He'd ever make a good carpenter. His dad thought he would. "You'll get there," he'd say: "Everyone needs to learn, no-one's perfect." He was so wise.

Then He was struck again by the thought that had plagued Him these past few years. Dad may be wise, but he didn't really understand. Mum did a little, but even she struggled. His mind went back to that first time He saw that look of bewilderment and frustration on her face and realised she didn't really understand Him.

She'd pushed through the crowd and yelled His name. To this day he wasn't sure whether it was in relief or anger. Probably a little of both. For the next few minutes she'd hugged Him tightly, totally oblivious of the crowds of dignitaries gathered around. She had either had her eyes shut or else she was just too relieved to care. He'd been wondering about her for four days by then, which is why He had been waiting in the temple. It seemed the obvious place to wait. Mum would know He was likely to be here.

But she didn't, and the look she gave Him, when eventually she relaxed, said more than that. The image of her face at that moment would stay with Him for ever. It spoke of days of anxiety; and as He looked into it He felt all the pain with her. It also spoke of love; a love which had imagined so much evil over the past few days. But, ultimately, it spoke of distance. As Jesus had looked into His mother's face, He knew she had not only not known He would be waiting here in the temple, she had also not understood why He should be here. His mother didn't really understand His relationship with His true Father.

Jesus pondered the significance of all His mother's face had said as they made the long three-day trek back to Galilee. They were in a crowd and Mum and Dad stuck close to His side with the rest of the family. They wouldn't let Him out of their sight. It felt as though He'd never had so much attention. But in a lot of ways it was the loneliest journey of His life. He worked through the implications of His logic again. If Mum couldn't understand His relationship with His Father, then how could Mum understand Him? It wasn't just an aspect of Him that His Mum couldn't

Perhaps she hadn't noticed. She smiled. She had noticed.

understand: it was Him.

Mary came out to look at Jesus' finger. She had that look of concern again, even though she'd seen a few dented carpenters' fingers in her time. She smiled and hugged Him and He realised how He loved her. But He knew she didn't really understand Him.[14]

The problems of being a Christian in a not-yet Christian home

The hardest place for most young people to be a Christian is at home. By and large, that seems to be true whether your family are Christians or not. Of course, though, it can be particularly hard if your parents aren't Christians. Sometimes such parents can be very supportive of you in your faith, even though they don't fully believe themselves. On the other hand, they can stubbornly refuse to listen to you, be hostile towards your faith or, worst of all, even ridicule you.

For your part you may feel almost alienated from them because there is such an important part of you they don't understand. You may also be frustrated by them because they won't listen or believe, and frustrated by yourself because you find it so hard to talk about your faith. Then, when you do talk, your actions let you down. It seems hard for you to make a stand at home, and harder still for your parents to accept what you're saying. Why?

1. The problem with your words
You may find it hard to talk about your faith for a number of reasons.

a. You may come from a family which doesn't talk about personal things, and that very much includes faith. So it is hard for you to start talking on this level. If you aren't conscious of Mum and Dad's embarrassment, you are of your own.

b. You may find your parents either don't or won't understand. They may turn everything into an intellectual argument or else pour scorn on it. They may resort to being patronising: "It's just a phase you're going through". This may be hard because they are cleverer arguers than you; hurtful because they are mocking something very important to you; or humiliating because they are treating you like a kid.

c. Perhaps most powerfully of all, though, you find it hard to talk about your faith at home because you find it hard to live as a Christian at home. If you don't *feel* a hypocrite, you may be reminded by your family that you *are* one! If actions speak louder than words, your words are so well and truly drowned that you might as well not bother with them.

2. The problem with your actions

Your parents will be watching you. This can be a positive thing as I'll come onto in a bit, but not always! Your parents are also quite prepared to write down everything you do and use it in evidence against you. There are three possible reasons for this:

a. They may be worried about your faith and its impact on you. They may actually find it oddly reassuring that you are still the same old sloppy, moody, lazy, messy child they've grown to know and, yes, love!

b. More likely they realise they have found a new lever to use on you to get their own way. That wonderful phrase: "If you call yourself a Christian ...", is such a powerful emotional tool. They know you want to witness. They know you will feel guilty about any form of failure. It is a strong parent who can resist the challenge of spiritual blackmail to get his or her own way! You're over a barrel and they may well know it!

c. Most likely of all, though, their complaints are valid! You can't write off all that your parents say as blackmail or persecution. Most of what they say will at least be based on fact and often they will kindly understate it. We've had teenagers live in our family for the last few years and so can balance what young people told us about the trials and persecutions of living with "pagan parents" with a bit of realism!

Be honest. Do you often rush in from school, yell for your food, eat it so quickly you only have time to comment on the fact the carrots weren't done, and disappear to ... the youth group prayer meeting or something? Mum is left behind staring at the debris of a meal she had worked hard over and hoped to enjoy a bit more. As she does, she makes a note mentally to add the washing up to the evening's chores of ironing, mending, pack lunch making and other unappreciated but demanded tasks.

You might say you're not like this. But the likelihood is that you do take your parents for granted and you are often insensitive, selfish and just plain sloppy. Everyone is to some degree and certainly most young people are. You might not mean to be; it's just that you just don't think. You might not want to be, but sometimes you're tired or rushed and it's the easiest option. And when you feel stressed, you snap, and you snap something awful! Well, it's home, you reason, and you need to relax somewhere. You don't like what you become, but have to admit that your parents do have a point. So this is why you cringe when you want to share your faith! Mum and Dad can't be conned by your words. They've seen the real you!

Then again, there is one area of life where actions speak even louder than in the home. Well, in your parents eyes they probably do anyway. In the classroom! I used to boast that young people who became Christians normally did better in their exams as a result. I don't any more. Too many can get so involved in spiritual things that earthly, fleshly pursuits, like A level Biology, are put to one side. What this tells a not-yet Christian parent, and I use my words carefully, is that becoming a Christian equals under-achievement. If these parents are cynical and worried about their young people's faith, I sometimes think they have good reason to be.

3. The problem with parents

There are other reasons too why parents either worry about your faith or seem hostile towards it.

a. They might not understand it. All they know is you've changed. Sometimes this change can be as dramatic as overnight. You've got religion! They may not know where you got it or how you got it, and they fear some sort of cult using indoctrination techniques may have influenced you. They may not understand what you've got and what it will mean. But as your parents they still feel responsible.

b. They may feel they're losing you. You are now out at church and other meetings a lot. You have a new influence on your life and this is an influence they don't understand. From their perspective your faith is something which has come between you and them. You may even feel this. You may feel that your faith is such an important part of you that if your parents can't understand it, then it is questionable whether they can really understand you at all. If you can feel this way, your parents can do too.

You will need to go out of your way to show that far from being a barrier between you all, your faith has given you a greater depth of love and appreciation for your family. This will involve an investment of time and energy, but it will be worthwhile for everyone.

c. Pride. Awkward, but true. Until now your parents have taught you. Now you are hoping to teach them about something as profound as the meaning of life! Most parents find this change of roles very hard to cope with, which seems quite understandable when you think about it. This is probably the main reason that preaching at Mum and Dad won't work. The best thing you can probably do is to introduce them to Christians nearer their age and who Mum and Dad might not feel so awkward about listening to.

d. Memories. It is just possible that your new-found faith may have brought back memories for Mum or Dad from the past. For some, these memories, for a whole host of reasons, may be bad, which prejudices them against the reality of your faith. For others, who have given up on a commitment they may have made in the past, your zeal and enthusiasm makes them feel guilty and uncomfortable.

The possibilities for sharing your faith at home

The good news, however, is that many parents are influenced and indeed converted by their children! In talking to parents who became Christians like this I found that two things in particular had made an impact.

1. The reality of their child's life

It can take a long time. You may need to endure all those "It's a phase you're going through"-type comments. But if you stick to it and your parents can see a difference, then they are likely to be impressed.

Reality shines through in the end. It is revealed in our attitude around the home. Parents are capable of picking up positives as well as negatives, even if it may not seem like it at the time. It is revealed in our attitude to school and in the way we think, talk and relate to people. In the end, even if your parents won't become Christians, they have to admit you have turned out well!

2. Your values and outlook on life

This, I discovered, was likely to have the second most powerful influence on parents. Of course, if you appear over-naive this can be counter-productive. But generally if you have high moral standards, a healthy, sensitive and balanced value of people and things, and a philosophy and outlook on life which is positive and attractive, then your parents will have to take note. Especially if they are only too aware that theirs is lacking!

So what should you do?

Let your life speak, and be creative and sensitive in letting it do so. Your actions can either build a foundation for your words or else cut the ground away from under them. Then again, your words are limited in any case. But a life that is starting to show love, joy, peace and all the other qualities of Jesus is attractive.

You may like to invite your parents to church so they can see what you are involved in. (This may be a good excuse for getting them along.) Do remember, though, that what you think is wild and brilliant, they may think is wild and weird! For instance, you may go to a church which has free worship and where anything goes. You probably love it. Mum and Dad, on the other hand, may be intimidated by the openness and lack of order as well as being put off by noise! Even so, they may still be able to see why it is good for you.

Above all, pray. Pray for yourself in your life at home. Pray for your parents that they will be open to hear, and pray that God will supply the people and opportunities to help them come to faith. This may in time involve you. It may not. Either way, it will probably take time.

A note on brothers and sisters

All these comments can, of course, just as easily apply to your brothers and sisters and other members of your family. Generally brothers and sisters might not find it so hard to learn from you, particularly if they are younger than you. They will, though, probably be more interested in your youth group and friends at first than the basis of your faith! So you may want to invite them out with your friends to social or youth group activities as the best way to start reaching out to them.

I'll finish this part, like others, with an honesty test to help you think through how best to live as a Christian in your family. First though, a quick look at those very practical problems various young people raised.

The practicalities of being a Christian in a not-yet Christian home

1. When you are worried about your family's apparent lack of faith

Most young people love their families very much. This love makes it very hard for Christian young people whose families haven't yet become Christians, especially when the youth group Bible study turns to the theme of heaven and hell. To be blunt, the thought of Mum or Dad suffering in the ways described in those horribly graphic illustrations of hell is enough to disturb anyone.

Hang on a moment, though. Just remember that if you're upset because you love Mum and Dad a lot and don't want to see them miss out on heaven, how much more distressed over them is God. After all He loves them perfectly. The truth is God doesn't want anyone to go to hell.[15] He just can't force them into heaven. Together, though, you can do all that's possible to give them the opportunity to understand God's love.

So when you pray for them, you aren't twisting the arm of an unwilling God: He's on your side! Remember particularly that it is very hard for Mum and Dad to learn everything about God from you. This means that one very practical way to pray is for God to bring other Christians into the lives of Mum, Dad, brother and sister. Never give up praying and hoping! God is the God of miracles who loves to answer prayer. It may take time! One great Christian of the last century recorded in his prayer diary how he prayed daily for someone for fifty years and he only became a Christian just before his death at the age of 93!

What's more, remember that we never really know what God has done in the lives of others. In other words, don't be too quick to write Mum and Dad off as pagans! They may be quieter or different in expression of their faith but this doesn't necessarily deny the reality of what has gone on in their hearts. Pray, trust and let God shine through you. That is all God asks of you and is the very most you can give to your family.

2. When a member of your family scorns or laughs at your faith

If this is happening to you, you probably find it very hurtful. The best thing to do is to think through why he or she is doing it. If it's a brother or sister it is very likely to be a case of immaturity and possibly insecurity too. He or she may not know how to react to you and your faith and so hits out. In this case you may notice he or she reacts similarly to other issues apart from your faith.

If it's Mum or Dad who are being hurtful, it is harder to take or explain. Certainly insecurity could be a cause here as well. Especially if a parent has had a Christian experience and given up. This could make them feel guilty or, if their experience of other Christians was a bad one they may feel resentful and worried for you. On the other hand, he or she may just be uneasy talking about anything too personal and there can be a whole host of reasons for that!

You will need to pray very hard that you don't react back, because that will just make matters worse. But it is perfectly fair to make whoever it is, aware of how hurtful they are being, though you'll need to do this in as calm a way as possible!

3. When your family don't live according to your new-found values

When Sarah became a Christian, she had a rather dramatic change in lifestyle and wardrobe! She didn't exactly become square. No-one could ever call Sarah that! But there was no doubt her values had radically altered. Unfortunately, her mum's hadn't!

Sarah's mum was living with a man and whereas before Sarah hadn't really been bothered, she now realised it wasn't right in God's eyes. Before she became a Christian, Sarah had never really thought marriage was important either. But now she saw it as the right way to have a fulfilled relationship and she was worried for her mum's happiness and security.

Sarah put her dilemma this way: "It was very hard and sometimes very embarrassing but just because my values changed, I couldn't expect everyone else's to do so, too. I couldn't change the whole structure of my family by voicing my new opinions in an aggressive way. In fact, I would more likely have alienated them. I needed to remember that God loved my family more than I could ever begin to imagine. So I needed to treat them with the same love and concern He had for them."

Sarah isn't saying you should condone actions and relationships you believe to be wrong. You should talk about how you feel, but you need to do so gently! Sometimes this is easier said than done! We all make mistakes and it is hard to hold your tongue when someone in your family is behaving in a way you think is wrong. It's all too easy to end up just making matters worse. At times like this, you need to have the humility to apologise and try to let your life speak. For instance, Sarah's mum's relationship eventually broke up very painfully. It was Sarah's willingness to listen and be there for her mum that gave her the chance to see God's love in action. As a result, Sarah was able to share her own beliefs through the experience. God is supremely in control of your family, and even if they seem the most godless lot, He really can change situations

4. When your family are very clever, or infuriating arguers, and make your beliefs sound stupid

Just remember Mum and Dad are more experienced and therefore probably more articulate than you, but this doesn't necessarily mean they are right, even if they sound it! What's more, you may be a young Christian and find it difficult to express exactly what you feel about your faith.

It is important, though, to be confident in your belief, and to hold to it, no matter what people say. There will be times when you feel totally crushed in what you believe and you need to work through your beliefs, preferably with an older Christian to help. This is definitely nothing to be afraid of. The whole process will actually make you stronger in your faith and clearer in your thinking. This means you will be able to help them more when you come to the next discussion with Mum and Dad.

Remember too that in the end it doesn't matter how many arguments your family throw at you, or for that matter how many you lose, they cannot argue with the way you live your life.[16]

5. When your family's plans clash with your church commitments

Most young people struggle to get enthusiastic about family outings, but two scenarios are particularly hard to cope with. The first is the Sunday trip to see granny or someone which is timed perfectly to clash with church. The second in some ways is even harder. For young people from broken families, weekends are often prime time to visit their other parent.

Obviously, this can just be a minor irritant as long as the clash doesn't occur too often, and then it is important to be as flexible and co-operative as possible. Being unreasonable over your desire to go to church is not the best impression with which to leave Mum and Dad.

The real problem occurs when there are expectations of you to be away every Sunday. You may find Mum and Dad more under-standing than you think though, and some compromise deal might be possible. Otherwise, you might find some alternative time to meet with other Christians, be it the church youth group, school Christian Union or something similar. The Bible tells us not to give up the habit of meeting together. It doesn't, though, insist we meet on a Sunday. The bigger problem occurs when your parents don't want you to attend any Christian activity at any time ...

6. When your parents oppose you in your faith

It is rare that parents will attack your faith itself, and anyway no one can stop you believing what you know in your heart to be true. What they are more likely to do is to stop you *practising* your faith. It probably won't be that they don't want you to go to any-thing. It might just be a particular church, event, holiday or mis-sion. It might be they don't want you to mix with a particular group of people. Ultimately, it might even be they don't want you to go in a certain direction such as to take a year off after school to do Christian work or go to Bible college or become a missionary.

First of all you will need to understand clearly why they are say-ing what they are. They may be right! You might need to cut down on activities if you are to get your exams. You might be doing too much and getting too tired. A particular group of people might not be a good influence on you. You might need to go on to sixth form, college or work before doing some Christian work or Bible train-ing. With their wider experience of judging character and making decisions, they might be able to see things clearer than you. Just because they aren't Christians doesn't mean their opinions are worthless! Listen to them.

If they are possibly or obviously wrong, the first thing to do is to be prepared to reason with them and compromise where neces-sary. Compromise is a sign of reasonableness, respect and matur-ity. Mum and Dad are more likely to trust you in the future if you display these qualities. Of course it may be Mum and Dad aren't willing to compromise! Then life gets harder.

At this point it might be time personally to withdraw a bit from the front line and bring others in to argue your case. If it's a church or event your parents are worried about, put them in touch with the minister, youth leader or organiser. I've had a number of worried parents ring me up about youth activities I've organised, and I can only remember one who remained unhappy with their child's involvement. The rest went away quite happy and a number have started coming to church themselves! Mum or Dad's tone often changes when talking to someone outside the family! Just being able to stress their point to someone else is often enough for them.

Of course, this isn't always true! Occasionally, and really it is very occasionally if you have followed my advice this far, they won't budge. The battle then becomes one you just can't seem to win. However, you can keep praying. My experience then is that God will either change your parents or even use the situation in ways no one could have anticipated. But if you want my answer to the hardest question of all, it is, yes, ultimately you should obey your parents. Not only because that is what the Bible says, but because it will be more hassle than it's worth long-term if you don't.

If you are over eighteen then you can legitimately, I believe, make your own decisions. But be very, very careful and take a lot of advice from mature folk before you go against your parents' wishes. It may be you will need to choose between God and Mum and Dad, but this is not a conclusion to come to quickly. It may still be better to obey them now even when you don't have to, in order to preserve your relationship with them in the future. I believe God honours people who are humble and patient enough to do so.

HONESTY TEST 7

Tick the box at the end of the statement which best describes you and your family.

1. **My parents**
   a. Are glad I'm a Christian and support me in my faith.   ❏
   b. Don't mind that I'm a Christian, but don't show much interest either.   ❏
   c. Are somewhat suspicious and uncertain of it.   ❏
   d. Don't like it or oppose it.   ❏

2. **I find it**
   a. Difficult to talk to my parents about my faith because I get embarrassed.   ❏
   b. Difficult because my parents put forward arguments which I can't answer, make jokes or are patronising.   ❏
   c. Impossible to talk about my faith.   ❏
   d. OK to talk about things. They'll listen.   ❏

3. **At home**
   a. I'm an argumentative slob and my parents hold it against me.   ❏
   b. My parents are out to get me and will pick up on the tiniest thing.   ❏
   c. I do my best and my parents have noticed a difference.   ❏
   d. I try from time to time to be considerate. I just don't always succeed.   ❏

4. **My brothers and sisters**
   a. Love to get at me and are totally disinterested in my faith.   ❏
   b. Are interested in my faith or have become Christians.   ❏
   c. Show some interest, but won't get too involved.   ❏
   d. Won't talk to me about it.   ❏
   e. Don't exist!   ❏

5. **Do your Mum and Dad support you in the Christian activities you are involved in and the plans you have for the future?**
   a. Yes.   ❏
   b. With some reservations.   ❏
   c. I don't tell them everything because I fear they won't understand or might not like it.   ❏
   d. No. We're battling over things.   ❏

(Turn to page 159 if you want to see how you scored.)

SECTION 4

Pressure points

This section looks at why the teenage years are so pressured. In particular it looks at pressure from:

Mum and Dad. How they can turn you into a nervous wreck because of their expectations, be it of your school work, your appearance, your friends, your musical or sporting talents or your future! How they can refuse to let you grow up and want at least to share in your decisions, if not make them, be over-restrictive and unacceptably nosey. How they can be frustrating due to their apparent lack of concern or personal motivation.

Peers. How to stand up to peer pressure and also win Mum and Dad's confidence and trust in your judgement.

It also looks at:

Arguments: what causes them; how to avoid them when they aren't necessary, and how to respond to them when they are.

Rebellion: how to regain trust and acceptance when you've messed up.

Growing pains

So they wanted to kill him. He had known they would be angry, but hoped it wouldn't come to this. For the second time in twenty-four hours Gideon was expecting to die. He shrunk down lower behind the woollen fleeces as he listened to his father arguing with the thugs outside. Somehow he felt secure, safe and warm behind these fleeces. He tucked his knees up under his chin, hugged them and wished, not for the first time, he was a little child again.

Life was so simple then. He was small enough to climb the olive trees at harvest time. He'd shake the fruit off for the rest of his family to collect in their cloaks below. It was fun. Last time he'd tried, however, a branch had snapped and he'd fallen on his sister. He could have killed her and he wasn't allowed up the olive trees again. Instead, as an adult he had the back-breaking job of picking the olives up from the ground. That wasn't fun.

When the grapes were ripe he'd pick and separate them. Most went to make wine, but the best he'd put to one side for the family. The very best, however, would get lost somewhere down his gullet. No one was supposed to know but everyone did and smiled at him because he was only a lad. Now they no longer smiled. "Gideon, you're not a boy any more. We're not having you make yourself sick on the best grapes."

Then, when the wheat was tall, he'd run through it pretending to chase off the enemy, the Midianites, and restore Israel to its rightful state. He was a hero. Now he was an adult and he really was being asked to restore Israel to its rightful state. He felt anything but a hero! Who knows what that angel would tell him to do next? Fight off the Midianites? Gideon crouched down lower behind the fleeces.

He remembered the last time he saw the angel. Only yesterday. He thought he was going to die then too. He felt so awkward, so worthless. He didn't know how to behave. He wasn't used to meeting angels. His dad would know what to do. But Gideon didn't. He hated being expected to cope in situations like this. But then he hated being treated like a child too ...

Despite himself, he had really quite enjoyed last night. It was exciting heading out on his own. He was scared silly while he was doing it, of course. But when he saw that smashed Asherah Pole, for the first time in his life he felt as though he had achieved something in his own right. It wasn't until he got back that he realised just how angry people might be. Within seconds all the excitement and confidence had drained out of him. Now here he was curled up in hiding while his dad sorted things out.

Gideon wished he understood himself. He longed for the excitement of being an adult, but feared the responsibility. He dreamt of being a hero, but felt like a wimp. He wanted independence, but here he lay, needing his dad more than any time in his life. Oh, messed up world![17]

The problems of being an adolescent canary

Growing up has always been tough, and not just for us, humans. Imagine what it must feel like to be a fledgling perched on the edge of the nest. You flap your wings and peer out. You know you ought to fly and you really want to. It's just that you've never done it before and you don't know whether you can. If you try, you might make an absolute mess of it. You feel awkward and nervous. Something inside tells you you've outgrown the nest and you need to step out on your own a bit more. But somehow you're also aware that it is a big, cold world out there and the nest then feels particularly secure and snug. Finally, you flop back into the nest again and in so doing bump into your sister flopping in from the other direction. A scrap follows over nothing at all and is only explainable in the light of the pent-up nervous energy and frustration felt by both of you.

I might be making a bit too much of this, but as a child, I used to breed canaries and always watched with interest the fledglings' first feeble flights! It looked quite comical to me, but it most certainly wasn't so funny for the bruised canary sitting dazed on the aviary floor.

The problems of being a young person

In a way, leaving the security of family is as terrifying for us as leaving the nest is for a fledgling. We may not need to learn to fly, but we do need to find our place in the social order. You may still be dependent on Mum and Dad, but you're sensing the need for a change in your relationships. It's time to become more independent. It is time to develop those relationships outside of the home which you will need to enjoy adult life to the full, first of all with God, but also with other people, and in particular your peers.

Something inside tells you you've outgrown the nest and you need to step out on your own a bit more.

The problem for most of us is that we can't believe anyone could possibly want to relate to us, value or accept us. We don't see much that's likeable about ourselves so why should anyone else? As we perch on the edge of the big, wide world, we fear we'll have no place in it. We really want to step out into it, but it's scary.

What's more, TV adverts and the like play on these feelings of inadequacy in order to make us buy their products. They claim that by buying them we can become acceptable to others. We try them and find we don't become beautiful or attractive like the people in the adverts, and this just makes us feel worse. The fault can't lie with the advert or product, we tell ourselves, so it must lie with us!

Then there are our friends' opinion of what we should do. And in our insecurity we daren't be different and so conform to what our friends and the media tells us. Yet this time, not only do we still fail to reach the mark, we also know we aren't being ourselves and one frustration or fear piles on top of another. Like the young canaries we flop back into the nest at the end of the day full of nervous energy and frustration. The result is often a fight with Mum, Dad, brother or sister over the silliest of things.

About this time home can become a kind of testing ground — a safe place in which we develop the confidence and strength of character we need to face the larger world. This isn't a bad thing. God intended it something like this, though without the fighting! Families are supposed to be the secure context to help us learn to stand on our own two feet. Our families are meant, first of all, to provide role models for us, and then the love and acceptance we need to try things, fail and try again and succeed.

The problem of growing up in your family

Unfortunately, it doesn't always work out like this. Perhaps Mum and Dad are hard to respect. Perhaps they smother and won't let you learn. Perhaps their love is deficient or badly expressed and instead of accepting you, they push you to become something you're not. They may be preoccupied or so damaged themselves they don't know how to encourage.

Of course, you might have very loving, together parents, but still feel really insecure. A major factor may be that these days Mum and Dad are no longer the greatest influence on our lives and their acceptance isn't necessarily enough. Media, including TV and the music and fashion industries, have a particularly strong influence on nearly all young people. And this media is controlled by vested interest groups who have their own benefit at heart, not yours. If your insecurity makes you vulnerable to their suggestions, so what, they think: it is in their interests that you should be insecure!

Now I don't want to put all the world's ills down to the media. TV, music and the like, can do a lot of good. But it does create an underlying need to keep up and to be very concerned with our appearance which adds to a sense of insecurity within everyone. This can make life difficult between friends at school, and, of course, with your family at home.

The urge to rebel

What I've said so far may help you to understand why you find yourself wanting to react or rebel against your family. Think of yourself like a drink mixer in which a cocktail of different emotions in varying proportions are being shaken up and you'll see why you sometimes want to break loose. The cocktail ingredients may include insecurity about the world you're facing, frustration or hurt about the family you're wanting to leave and, of course, just plain old-fashioned inquisitiveness.

If you've been brought up in a certain way, you will want to know what it's like living in a different way. If you don't feel free to find out, you may start to resent the values, lifestyle and principles you've been brought up with. It may be your family's wealth or poverty, their mundaneness or eccentricity, their faith or lack of it, their strictness or looseness that gets you frothing. Or perhaps it's their stifling closeness or risky independence, their too high expectations or total lack of ambition that makes you want to explode from the bottle and shower a little of your feelings over everyone.

The fact you may not feel like rebelling may just be that you have done well under the system. You've found a position in which people accept, value and relate to you. Alternatively, it may be that you are too crushed and haven't the spirit left to rebel. Rebellion in itself is not a good or bad thing. What makes it good or bad is what we rebel against and how.

The purpose of this section is to help you understand yourself better in the light of pressure from your parents and your peers. It will cover such areas as parents' expectations of your education, behaviour, success, career and relationships and we'll consider their ability or failure to let you grow up in a secure way. It will also look at how pressure from friends to conform in ways that deeply worry Mum and Dad create extra stress points at home.

Then it will answer how to react to these pressures with special reference to that favourite domestic pastime: the family argument. Finally, some advice on how to sort your life out after you've messed up! Let's start, though, by looking at the pressures Mum and Dad put on you.

Pressure from parents

"We've spent so much money on you and look where it's got you!" The words still rang in Ruth's ears. She could cope with them better now she was older and had become a Christian. In the past it had taken drugs and sheer will-power to help her handle them. Both had left their mark.

Ruth thought back again to one of her earliest memories. She sat with Dad staring at a wooden toy clock. Dad was getting more and more worked up over her inability to learn how to tell the time. In the end he resorted to hitting her.

She remembered her first tour with the orchestra. She was nine or ten. She couldn't be sure which any more. All she knew was that she was very young. She felt so nervous about being away from home and performing in front of so many people, and it obviously showed. Her parents got a letter from the tour leader to say she hadn't been up to standard and wouldn't be required on the next tour. She would never forget her parents' anger with her.

She remembered first taking Betablockers at fifteen. She hadn't lost her fear of performing, but nor had her parents lost their determination that she should do so. They recommended the drugs to help calm her down.

Everything she did, everywhere she went, everyone she met involved pressure. She was never allowed as a child to sit down at home and do nothing. She was always under orders to be working at something. When she went out with Mum, meeting people was a trial. Even now Mum would prod her and say "Go and say thank you." It made it so hard to be natural. Her mum didn't have faith in her in the smallest thing.

It was hardly surprising that she had withdrawn into herself. She couldn't concentrate. She had become nervous and shy. Even saying "Hello" was hard. At social gatherings she'd feel self-conscious, freeze and her face would start twitching. Often she'd get ill with stress.

Her brother had responded rebelliously. He felt the pressure, too, and was frequently in hospital because of his nerves. He'd only coped finally by breaking away from the family and doing his best to shock Mum and Dad. Her way of coping had been different.

At first she'd gritted her teeth and driven herself to overcome the fears. Going shopping alone had become a torturous ordeal, so she targeted it as a fear to overcome. Every day she would force herself to go into town. This tactic was all right up to a point, but it didn't take the feelings away. She needed to become a Christian before those could be dealt with in any meaningful way. And Ruth knew she was a living testimony to the truth that prayer can change things.

But the problem itself hadn't gone away. She had been reminded of that by Mum's repetition yet again of those haunting words which had set off this train of thought. Even now she felt tense with people. Even now she was so conscious of all that her parents had given her and felt their pressure to "produce the goods". Even now she felt guilty if she just did her own thing. Even now when she thought about it all, she wanted to chuck in whatever she was doing and would feel her energy and joy in life draining away. Even now when she was twenty-one.

In the stories I've been telling in this book, I've changed facts here and there to conceal identities, and to be honest this has been a fun thing to do! There have been many times, though, when I wished I could just as easily change the facts in the real life situations. But I can't: they have to be accepted, faced up to and overcome through considerable pain.

Ruth was one of those who let me tell her story as it was, without changes. She is also one of those who has been able to face up to the trauma and come out the other end, scarred but whole. She is an example of how Jesus can make a difference in what may seem impossible situations. This is why I wanted to tell her story. Not because it's extreme; it probably isn't that unusual. But because it's a story of hope.

Most young people feel pressure from parents in one form or other, and often it's a good thing they do. This part will help you understand the more common brands of parent pressure better and know how to respond to them. However a number of young people feel under an intense pressure which is anything but help-ful. If this is your situation, I want to encourage you. There is hope in Christ. You may still feel twinges of pain, but you needn't go through life broken or resentful.

The young people I talked to, highlighted ten different ways Mum and Dad can put pressure on you, and that doesn't include the one we've already looked at: the pressure to be a Christian! Be warned, when you've read these next few pages you may decide that your mum and dad aren't that bad after all! They may be infuriating, boring or just plain odd but they could be worse! On the other hand, you may end up saying a big *yes* to some of these pressures; in which case you can go on to read why Mum and Dad might be like this and also most importantly how to cope with them! What's more, through all these pressures we'll see there is a Perfect Parent who stands over you, loves you and helps you in an incredibly practical way.

The top ten parental pressures

1. Pushing too hard at school/college. For instance, by want-ing you to do more and more homework. You may appreciate some pressure but they're over the top. They might keep causing a fuss at school and now you are scared to tell them how much homework you've really got, in case they send another letter to your teacher!

2. Thinking you're cleverer than you really are. Most parents like to think their dogs and kids are smart. To admit otherwise can be a slur on them! The smartness or achievements of your brother or sister may be used in evidence against you, and this certainly isn't helpful! Mum and Dad may be high achievers themselves and can't see how it could possibly be that you aren't. I'm not say-ing you're stupid or anything. You're just not Mastermind!

3. Having their own set plans for your education. They may have plans for you to stay on at school or go to college, and may even want you to take certain options. Now don't get me wrong. You probably want to achieve, do your best and possibly go on to college or something. But Mum and Dad's pressure doesn't neces-sarily help you in this.

4. Having an unwritten dress and appearance code. If you're a girl, comments may be made about your dress or the fact you don't often wear one! Hairstyles, earrings and make-up are also

Comments may be made about your dress or the fact you don't often wear one!

points of contention. Boys generally have an easier time, but may still battle over similar things. Of course, nothing may be said. It's more what isn't said which counts. Silence is golden — and guilt-edged!

5. Having expectations of your attitudes and actions. Family custom may dictate you do certain things in a certain way. You visit granny on the third Sunday of every month, and when you do, you wear the prescribed clothes, behave and talk about things in a set way. You go on the family walking holiday and enjoy it. You don't question certain taboo subjects. You don't like certain types of music and if you do, you have to play them at snooze level when Mum and Dad are around. The possibilities are as varied as are family customs!

6. The right type of friends! Parents realise the effect friends can have on you and will, subtly or obviously, want to influence the choice of friends who influence you.

7. Having the right interests. Music, sport, or hobbies all may be encouraged, or discouraged, to the point of obsession.

8. Career. This may have been determined before you were born, set either by Mum or Dad's personal dreams or by family tradition. The army and the church used to be the expected professions for respectable children in Britain. Today it can be the law and medicine! Fine if you share these ambitions, tricky if you don't.

9. Mothering or smothering! In your darker moments you wonder whether you will spend the rest of your life as Mummy or Daddy's little boy or girl. Why can't they give you any space? Why can't they allow you any privacy? They want to be in on all your decisions, if not making them for you. They fire questions at you and want more answers than you're prepared to give. They take initiatives and intervene without being asked.

They may expect, as of right, first refusal of your time so that you need to fit your own life around family events. They may like to do things with you, such as going to the doctor's or for an interview. They may enter your room at will. They may like to meet your friends when they come around and talk endlessly to them. They may even read your post. To put it bluntly, they don't seem to trust you and want to run your life for you.

10. Not appearing to care for you. Amazing as it seems, there are some who will have read these top nine pressures and thought: "If only ... !" If you are one of these, your problems are the very reverse. Your parents may not so much believe you are a genius, as an idiot. There may be no tradition of further education in your family and no help for you in attempting to get it. You may not be so much smothered as shoved out! For reasons best known to Mum and Dad, they don't seem to care or else are unaware of your need of them and their encouragement.

The causes of the problems

There are a number of reasons why parents expect things of their children.

1. Love. Obviously, not all expectations and pressures are bad. Most young people admit to needing pressure and are grateful for it. Most also admit their goals are at least similar to their parents' and without their help they wouldn't achieve them. One revealing fact I discovered was that as many young people complain that their parents didn't push them enough as complain of being pushed too hard. Expectations and wanting the best for a child is a sign of Mum or Dad's love.

Of course, that love can be badly expressed or misplaced. It may be your parents think they are helping when their pushing is actually breaking you. It doesn't help either if Mum and Dad seem to love their own idea of you and not you as you really are. In other words they simply won't accept you as you with the gifts and personality you have, but seem set on changing you into someone you're not. Then again over-protectiveness is also often the result of badly expressed love. Mum or Dad, may not be able to see that their love is crippling you.

2. Social pride. Parents suffer from parental and peer pressure, just like you. There may be unspoken rules in your family or social or church group which Mum and Dad feel they need to stick to in order to keep up appearances. These expectations may become such an obsession that they can end up being more important than your happiness or well-being. As with any obsession, the people who have it are usually the last to spot it!

3. The second chance. Where Mum or Dad has missed out on an opportunity to do something, they may be overkeen to make sure you don't miss out too. This may be generated by love and involve sacrifice. But what Mum or Dad fail to see in their determination, is that although they may want you to have this opportunity, you don't share their enthusiasm! Another possibility is that Mum and Dad may simply want to re-live that opportunity through you, regardless of how you feel about it.

4. The joy of parenting. "What?" you say. Yes, the amazing truth is that Mum and Dad may have enjoyed parenting you as a child so much that they don't want to lose you. They may find a lot of their meaning in you and don't want to let you go. They've spent so many hours feeding, nursing protecting and taking an interest in you that stepping back is hard, even frightening.

5. Plain bad parenting. Finally, a few parents really are just lousy mums and dads. Sophie told me honestly that she felt her mum just wasn't cut out for being a parent and she was far more interested in a career. Sophie could point to various examples of apparent carelessness or thoughtlessness to back up her opinion. Be careful, though, about jumping to this conclusion. Mums and dads like this are rarer than we're sometimes tempted to imagine.

The effects of pressure on you

You may rise to the challenge and do well under pressure. But beware that you don't lose a sense of perspective and balance in the process. Encouragement to do well in your education and career can lead to you overvaluing these things. Don't get me wrong. They are important, but not as important as knowing how to relate to God and to other people. You may end up with great qualifications and an excellent job, but be unable to appreciate your husband or wife, or have few friendships that have any depth. On the other hand, you may feel the hurdles are too high and end up stressed, lacking in confidence or resentful and rebellious.

In particular, if you feel over-mothered or smothered, you've probably been wrestling either with the temptation to rebel or to submit. If you rebel you may throw the baby out with the bath water. In other words deliberately decide against some things which you would enjoy or benefit from in order to make a statement to Mum. If you submit, you also can do so at a cost. If you keep giving in, you might in time find it harder to run your own life and make your own decisions.

You may be caught somewhere between these two temptations.

You get frustrated with Mum or Dad trying to run your life for you but you feel guilty when you confront them because you know they love you and can see they are hurt. They have you over a barrel by a use of emotional blackmail so subtle even they don't recognise they're using it.

You may also have quite specific problems to cope with, such as:

Criticism. There is often little logic behind some mum's and dad's criticism and lack of trust or belief in their children. Whatever problems there are probably have more to do with them than you! The trouble is it's you who suffers. If you are at the receiving end of lack of encouragement or criticism, you may be tempted to do one of two things: either to try desperately hard to win approval or else give up. Either way you can get very bitter.

Frustration. Parents who don't understand you can be very frustrating. You may long for parents who shared your dreams and at times insisted you knuckled down to work. You may be tempted to despise parents who don't seem to share your ambition and drive and who appear to be content to do nothing with their lives.

Freedom. The last pressure represents the other extreme of the ones we've talked about so far. Instead of parental expectations, you're left to do whatever you want with life. Instead of being smothered you're shoved out into the big wide world to stand on your own two feet.

Anyway enough of the woes, now its time to think about how to face up to these pressures.

Responding under pressure

1. Be honest about your feelings

Which were the top ten parental pressures you were nodding your head to? Whichever they were, it is important that you talk to Mum and Dad about them. This is an opportunity to get these things off your chest, and for both sides to understand each other better.

When challenged about expectations for their children, most parents claim all they really want is for them to be happy.

Somehow the message has got distorted in transmission. You may even have misunderstood what your parents' true hopes for you are.

One lad I know, went off to college recently very unhappily. He only went because he was convinced that it was what his parents required. In fact they had told him all they wanted was for him to be happy and he needn't go if he didn't want to. He just didn't believe them! His dad's family always went to university and he couldn't believe they didn't expect him to do so to.

Midway through the first term he came home very unhappy and had to decide whether to go back or give up. When he talked with his parents, they again told him he didn't need to go back. They just wanted him to be happy. This time the light dawned. He realised that what they had said was what they meant. They really *didn't* expect him to struggle through college if his heart wasn't in it. Talking came as something of a relief, as you can imagine. It can be so eye-opening for both you and Mum and Dad when you know what really is expected.

Talking can also make Mum and Dad more aware of the pressures you feel. Many parents just haven't a clue about the stresses their expectations place on you, and the hurts you feel because of their requirements. For instance, some family traditions may be so much second nature to Mum and Dad that it wouldn't occur to them that you could find them pressurising. They won't understand either, unless you talk about them.

Mum and Dad may also be encouraging you in the right things but in unhelpful ways. Let's face it, it's often not so much the expectations which hurt but the way they are communicated! With all the love in the world your parents might not see what they are doing to you ... unless you tell them.

Sometimes Mum and Dad push you because they are concerned that you don't seem to be pushing yourself. If they don't push, they reason, no one else will and you'll get nowhere. If you share some of your own dreams with them, they will see that you do have goals and ideas of your own on how to use your talents. This will encourage them hopefully to have more belief in you.

Of course, they may not like all the dreams you share and you may need to be ready to compromise. That may sound hard, but in the end you may find out your parents weren't as daft as they first appeared. You may also find them more willing to compromise and trust you in other areas.

Then again, if you're feeling smothered, by talking you may be able to help Mum and Dad see how they are hurting you. Alternatively, you might see that what you perceived to be over-protectiveness wasn't as unreasonable as you first thought!

2. Bring in outside help

However prepared you are to talk, dream and compromise, Mum or Dad may not be so willing. Then you will need help. Your other parent may be more rational and balanced and perhaps you could appeal to him or her. A brother or sister may be able to put your case, perhaps from their own experience. A teacher may be able to talk to Mum or Dad about realistic expectations or work levels. Someone from a relevant career may be able to enthuse Mum and Dad about the possibilities for your future. And so on.

Even then Mum and Dad may not be inclined to listen. In this case, please don't bottle up your fears and feelings. You must find someone to affirm you in who you are and advise you in what to do. It may be a youth leader or someone from church, a friend's mum, or an older brother or sister. Preferably, though, it should be someone mature.

As far as smotherers go, my gut feeling is that most care enough for you that when you tell them what you feel, they will listen. Unfortunately, though a number of smotherers are so emotionally damaged themselves for one reason or another, they will find it very find to hear what you are really saying. They may take it personally or just not grasp or accept your point at all. This can be very frustrating! I know some of you will be nodding furiously at this point! If you are, you need to bring in outside help.

Once again in the case of a smothering Mum or Dad, you may be able to turn to your other parent or a brother or sister for support. Going outside the family may be taken personally by Mum or Dad but may be necessary if you are to get the problem sorted without ending up a rebel or a recluse! At least find someone you can talk to. Get the feelings out of your system and some helpful advice into the situation.

If you face loads of criticism from Mum or Dad it is particularly important you find someone to encourage you. You can face criticism so much easier when you know that someone somewhere appreciates you. They might also encourage you enough so that you are able to talk calmly with Mum or Dad or they may be sensitive or close enough to Mum and Dad to chat with them themselves.

Finding someone who understands you or to whom you can

turn is also important if you feel frustrated by lack of understanding at home or feel left to stand on your own two feet. Such a person can be your first matter for prayer!

3. Pray

God is the perfect Father who both protects and trusts us. He understands us and all our feelings. Ultimately He can keep you sane. He is the God of the impossible. He can even change Mum and Dad, their attitudes and expectations. In the meantime He can heal the hurts of the past and supply all the patience, wisdom and firmness you require for the present. It may take time, but even for someone like Ruth, to whom I introduced you at the beginning of the chapter, prayer really did change things.

The Bible has so much to say about what it means to have God as a Father. He has plans for you, to prosper you and not to hinder you.[18] He will always accept you as you are, believe in you, dream for you and help you know a wholeness and fulness in life.[19] He promises to watch over you as a mother eagle watches over her young.[20] In other words, He allows you freedom and trusts you but will never leave you and always be there for you.[21]

There are as many types of hurts as there are people, and I am conscious that these few pages only touched on a few problems. You may like to think through your own situation a bit more before moving on and I've provided an honesty test on the opposite page to help you in that. After that the next set of pressure points I'll look at are those which come from your own age group.

HONESTY TEST 8

Tick the box at the end of the statement which best describes your situation.

1. In the way your parents express concern, are they
    a. Overprotective? ❑
    b. Under-protective? ❑
    c. About right? ❑
    d. Occasionally irritating, but normally OK? ❑

2. In their encouragement of you in your schoolwork, are they
    a. Seemingly disinterested? ❑
    b. Encouraging, interested and sensitive? ❑
    c. A little too pushy and embarrassing but generally OK? ❑
    d. Over pushy? ❑

3. What dreams do your parents have for you?
    a. They encourage me to dream, but they have no set plans for me themselves. ❑
    b. They don't say much, but I think they have certain expectations. ❑
    c. They have said what they want me to do with my life. ❑
    d. They don't expect me to amount to much. ❑

4. Do you feel there are certain expectations of dress and behaviour in your family which you don't find helpful?
    a. Yes. ❑
    b. Sometimes. ❑
    c. No: I'm free to be myself. ❑
    d. No: We don't have that close a family. ❑

5. Do you feel your parents give you enough trust and freedom?
    a. Sometimes. ❑
    b. No. ❑
    c. Too much. It sometimes appears they don't care. ❑
    d. About right. ❑

6. Do you ever feel either of your parents are regularly and unjustifiably critical and negative about you?
    a. No. ❑
    b. Occasionally. ❑
    c. Yes. ❑

(Turn to page 159 if you want to find out how you scored.)

Peer pressure

Lisa closed the front door as quietly as she could and crept down the hall. She was late and knew it. With any luck though, Mum and Dad would be in bed and they wouldn't know the precise time she'd come in. If they asked, she'd tell them. She'd also tell them why. Taxi drivers sometimes seemed as reliable as the British weather — and about as pleasant! Still she'd enjoyed her extra forty-five minutes at the party. It had been a real riot, and thanks to that miserable lifeform who had driven her home, she had a good excuse.

She slipped her arm through the doorway to the left to turn off the kitchen light — there'd be no time for a late drink now. But as she did so she sensed something, someone was there. It was either bad news, very bad news or worse. It could either be a chain saw murderer, the monster which she as a kid used to believe lived behind the cooker ... or Mum.

It was Mum. And she was very upset.

Mum looked up at her "little girl" who now stood in the doorway. The hall light appeared as a glow around her. She would have looked the perfect angel just a year ago with her long blond hair and in her school uniform. Now she looked more like a "Hells Angel". Her hair had changed colour with the seasons, and very odd coloured seasons they were too. Her clothes were still uniform, just different that's all. The school blazer had been replaced by leathers. All that was left of a skirt it seemed was the belt. The tights were most certainly non-regulation. Jewellery hung from her like tinsel on a Christmas tree. Oh Lisa ...

Now Anna was different. She always dressed so sensibly. They never argued. She looked and played the part of the perfect daughter. How could two parents have raised two totally different children? Where on earth did they go wrong?

One they could trust. She was sensible and thought things through to their logical conclusions. She had a depth to her. She felt deeply, thought deeply, cared deeply. The other was a constant worry. She was driven by impulse and jumped into things without thinking. She was superficial, gullible, fickle and selfish. She was heading for trouble, Mum knew it. Whenever she went out, Mum always feared the worst.

"I'm sorry I'm late. Don't get upset." The words seemed to

creep into Mum's head by the back door and it took a while for her to register them and a while longer to respond. She looked up slowly and uttered tiredly:

"Oh Lisa ... you know its not you I worry about. It's your sister."

Lisa and Anna's mum was right. If either was going to get into trouble, it would be Anna not Lisa. And it was. Anna is older than Lisa, but age isn't that important really. Anna looks more sensible than Lisa, but looks can be deceptive. What really counts is what's going on inside. In other words, which girl thinks things through and which just jumps in? Which girl has strong values and opinions of her own and which is easily led by others? Which girl can see things in perspective and which is easily dazzled and infatuated by whoever comes along? Which girl understands life and which just lets it happen?

Lisa has had a string of boyfriends much older than herself but has handled them. Anna has had fewer and been hurt so much more, sexually, emotionally and physically. It's no good Anna complaining to her mum that she is older than Lisa or more sensibly dressed or even that she argues less. Mum will worry, and rightly so.

Of course, some mums would worry overmuch about Lisa too. They would worry about what the neighbours say when they see her dressed the way she is. They would worry about what the family might say about her boyfriends. They might just worry by force of habit. Lisa, though, gives Mum fewer reasonable grounds for worry.

Mum knows Lisa has some odd boyfriends but also knows she has strong views on the place of sex in relationships. Mum knows Lisa goes to some odd places, but she also knows she will think before acting and is therefore less likely to walk home late and alone, get a lift with someone she doesn't know or stay somewhere when things get hot! Mum knows Lisa meets some odd people, but she also knows she has strong enough views about alcohol and drugs not to be easily led.

Of course, Lisa is still at risk. A boyfriend can always be a wolf in sheep's clothing. She can be let down and have trouble getting home. Trouble may brew up where she is before she has chance to get out. Someone could lace a drink. Her mum will always be anxious about things beyond her daughter's control. But deep down she trusts Lisa because she knows she has a "depth" to her.

You can't tell someone with "depth" by their age or by their appearance. You can get some idea by the way they talk and more by the way they act. It is a magic ingredient which includes a number of qualities such as common sense, sensitivity, logic, strong values, good judgement of character and a sense of perspective. Some have it from a very early age. Some never seem to acquire it. You will need it if you are to get on not only with Mum and Dad, but also with life.

Depth comes as you learn to think things through. You work out carefully what you believe in and then stick to it. If you decide to change your views, you only do so after talking with a number of people you respect. You work out carefully what all the results of your actions will be before you take them. It doesn't stop you having fun. It just makes sure it really will be fun, long-term.

Developing depth also teaches you to work out who can be trusted and who can't. Finally, you are able to see what really counts in life. You feel deeply. You understand the value of things and know what to treat lightly and what to treasure. You have some sense of direction and purpose.

The importance of demonstrating that you have an inner depth and strength becomes obvious when we look at how Mum and Dad can view your friends and their influence on you.

What goes through your mum's head when she thinks about ...

1. Your friends

Mum knows all about the power of peer pressure, and the possible impact of bad influences! She will be particularly concerned if you have shown yourself in the past to have been gullible or if you have had no experience of friends like this before. She knows how easy it is for our judgement to be dazzled by people who are different and exciting. She will fear their influence on you.

On the other hand, if she knows you are a pretty good judge of character, have some understanding of the world around you, aren't easily conned and are even harder to sway, then she'll be happier. She will still worry. She might wonder, when you are supposed to be such a good judge of character, why you are mixing with some people. She is, though, more likely to give you the benefit of the doubt rather than judge your friends too quickly by outward appearances.

2. Boy/girlfriends

Mum knows all about the power of first or early love. She will be particularly concerned if her daughter suddenly produces a first boyfriend much older than her. She will fear you are responding to attention, any attention from anyone, which you may not have been shown before. She will fear that the excitement and novelty of it will dazzle you. She will obviously be suspicious of his intentions. She will fear love at any stage might blind you. She will fear that you might not be thinking logically. She will fear whether you are able to identify true love.

On the other hand if she knows you have high standards concerning relationships and the place of sex, then she'll be happier. She will want to understand what the basis of your friendship is and allay any fears she has.

We've stressed talking a lot so why not set Mum's fears at rest and say why you like him. You may even enjoy the chat!

One stage on, when considering marriage the same principles apply. Early marriage or marriage to a considerable older partner is obviously a concern to caring parents. They will probably be more at ease if they can be sure you've thought through your decision and it hasn't been an impulsive whim. It won't remove all the doubts and questions, but it certainly eases them.

3. Activities

Mum knows all the horror stories which are told about parties, concerts and young peoples' sleep-overs and holidays. She will be concerned about sex, drugs, alcohol and violence. She was young once. She remembers the excitement and curiosity of sex. She might remember what it felt like to be aroused for the first time, though she probably hasn't told you! She knows the temptation to try things you've never tried before, especially when all your friends are trying it. She can remember the daft things which go on and the pranks which sometimes go wrong. She quite possibly remembers making impulsive decisions, like walking home alone, and regretting them later, though she probably never told her parents!

On the other hand, if she knows you tend to think things through, don't take silly risks and have strong opinions about sex, alcohol and drugs, then she will be happier. She will still worry about things beyond your control. But she is more likely to trust you and not immediately say NO!

Proving yourself responsible

1. Acquiring depth

I hope by now you can see that being responsible is not really an outward thing. That might be more to do with being respectable than responsible. It's an inward thing, which is why I've avoided until now using the word "responsible", which you might mis-understand. Instead I have used the word "depth". I hope I've explained clearly enough what I mean by it and you can see that it doesn't equal boredom!

Being a Christian is a great way of acquiring depth. God shows us what counts, what is right, how to live life to the full. As one psalmist put it, His depth calls to our depth.[22] He draws out depth. We become stronger, more secure and together people. When we find depth in our relationship with God, then we seem to be able to enjoy everything that much more.

2. Communicating depth

If your parents are to be able to trust your common sense, they need to know about it. You can build trust by talking about how you think and feel with them. If you don't do so, they have less reason to believe you are trustworthy. You also need to demon-strate that common sense in action as much as possible. You'll make mistakes, but then your parents made them when they were young and would admit to making them still, if they are honest! The important thing is that the majority of your life demonstrates a consistency and stability.

This is particularly important if your interests and opinions dif-fer from your parents. Lisa certainly doesn't dress in the way her mum would! But this doesn't bother Mum because she knows that

Lisa, despite her eccentricities, is trustworthy.

Of course there are more important issues about which your views might differ from your parents. If your friends, or more particularly your boy or girlfriends, aren't Christians, this will probably worry your parents, if they are Christians themselves; even if it doesn't worry you. It will help if they know they can trust you, but they will still be anxious, and I must admit I believe rightly so! Then again there are fundamental areas where your disagreement will probably be seen by Mum and Dad as evidence that you don't think things through. If you have a more relaxed view of sex, they aren't so likely to be unconcerned as you poke your head around the living room door to say good-bye on your way out to the party.

Of course, not all parents are reasonable. Yours may not be prepared to trust or credit you with any intelligence at all. Outward appearances may mean everything to them and they may seem to worry more about what people will think of them than for you. If you feel your mum and dad are somewhat like that then the next part might interest you. It's all about those times when the pressure gets too much and the arguments begin. But first ...

THE BIG, BIG HONESTY TEST

After each statement tick the box which best describes you.

1. **Would you say you had strong views and values?**
   a. Yes. ❏
   b. On some things. ❏
   c. On a few things. ❏
   d. Not really. ❏

2. **Are your views easily swayed and are you easily led?**
   a. Sometimes. ❏
   b. Quite a lot, I suppose. ❏
   c. Yes, to be honest. ❏
   d. No. ❏

3. **Would you say you are a good judge of character?**
   a. No, I can be a bit naive. ❏
   b. I sometimes can be a soft touch! ❏
   c. Yes. ❏
   d. Most of the time. ❏

4. **Are you prone to making impulsive decisions?**
   a. Yes. ❏
   b. No. ❏
   c. Only at my very maddest! ❏
   d. Sometimes. ❏

5. **Do you think a lot about what your priorities should be, what counts most in life and how you are going to make the most of it?**
   a. Yes, and I know what I want out of life. ❏
   b. Quite a lot and, I feel deeply about some things. ❏
   c. Sometimes I do. ❏
   d. Not really, I just get on with it, to be honest. ❏

6. **Do you ever talk to your parents about your thoughts, feelings and values?**
   a. Sometimes, but not often. ❏
   b. Rarely. We're not that sort of family. ❏
   c. Never. ❏
   d. Yes, often. ❏

(Turn to page 159 if you want to know how you scored.)

Fighting for peace

Arguments and how to avoid them

The Bible is full of family arguments. Cain and Abel, Jacob and Esau, Joseph and his brothers. In the New Testament we are introduced to a pair of brothers called the Sons of Thunder. They were both capable of a world-class sulk when things didn't go their way. They showed this when they threw a little tantrum on leaving a town which didn't receive them as well as they would have liked.(23) They showed strong signs of being spoilt and turned to Mum when they wanted something. So, for instance, Mum went to Jesus with requests on their behalf!(24) Can you imagine what it must have been like living in their house as they grew up! Perhaps that is one of the reasons they got their nicknames: Sons of Thunder! It could have been their next-door neighbour who first suggested the names to Jesus!

The Bible is full of family arguments because the world is full of families! That is the great thing about the Bible. It's God's Word addressing very practical issues in our lives. In a bit we'll look at what the Bible says about sorting out arguments. But first, let's think about why they happen.

The causes of family arguments

I've carried out a small poll among young people I chatted with, to find out what caused the most arguments between them and their parents and secondly, between them and their brothers and sisters.

In the parent poll straight in at number three came "Curfew Times", at two "Money Trouble", but the number one argument was without doubt "The Bedroom Mess"! Meanwhile, in the sibling poll, a surprise number three argument "The Food Debate", at number two "TV Programmes" just squeezed out of the top spot by "That's my jumper!" — a compilation of clothing arguments!

Other flashpoints included irritation and frustration with Dad for his awful jokes, his patronising manner and basic insensitivity; with Mum, for her nosiness, non-stop chatter (especially when the TV's on) and fussiness; and with brother and sister for their messiness, music and slobiness! There seem to be as many potential causes for arguments as people!

Actually though, these aren't really the causes of arguments but normally just the excuses for them. The real causes lie a little deeper. First of all there's living on top of each other. By the law of averages, the more time you spend together with anyone, the more likely you are to get on each other's nerves. You may only need five minutes of your brother's company to get wound up. But five minutes, five hours, it doesn't matter which. Sooner or later he will achieve his goal and you'll go mad! Which brings me neatly onto the next point.

You may actually want to argue. Nothing suits some people better than a good blow up. In fact you may be really frustrated because your parents never argue. Some characters seem to need a good argument to clear the air. This may not make you any less godly than those who never argue. They just might be sulkers and save all their feelings for an internal stew. In the end it doesn't make much difference whether your bitterness is held in or is let rip with all its fury. God sees the heart anyway.

Brother, sister or even you may enjoy a good argument because you know you can win it! After a day away at school losing every argument in sight, it puts your self confidence back into shape to score that home victory even if it's over poor, defenceless little brother.

Mums and dads, brothers and sisters are also good to argue with because, lets face it, they haven't got much choice. They have to live with you. If you're obnoxious to your friends, they can dump you. Your poor old family can't.

Finally, everyone tends to come home tired. You're all making no effort. You've been nice all day. Now you want to be a miserable slob and enjoy it. What happens when four or five irritable, if not miserable, slobs get together? You probably don't need me to answer this question for you!

Arguments and how to avoid them

Now you may think from what I've said so far that I think arguments are a good idea. Well, that's not quite true. But I do think it's better to be honest about your feelings than stew on them! Furthermore Jesus may have told us we should be peace-makers,[25] and Paul may have told us we shouldn't let the sun go down on our anger,[26] but neither said we should never get angry or confront people. Jesus and Paul did both these things!

What Jesus was particularly concerned about was that we should become people who wanted to create peace and didn't delight in arguments for argument's sake. And Paul wasn't saying we should never get angry, but we should be honest about our feelings and then forgive and make up, not letting our anger boil away inside us to blow up in a really harmful and uncontrollable way! Practically, this might mean actually letting the sun go down on your anger! Let me give you an example:

You get in from being out late and find your favourite jumper lying on the floor halfway up the stairs. You'd told your sister she wasn't allowed to wear it. You needed it in a couple of days and had meant to put it in the wash that evening. But she'd obviously ignored you. She'd been so highly strung that evening that nothing would have surprised you. But just because things weren't right between her and her boyfriend, that doesn't give her the right to do as she pleases. You'll have to say something or she'll think she can get away with it. Being a Christian, you decide that instead of a full-blown yell, you'll just put your head around the corner of the living room door and make a sarcastic comment.

When you do, you get yelled out of court by your sister, your mum turns on you and your dad mutters something about "Call yourself a Christian ..." Even the dog raises his eyebrows as if to say, "You really blew that, didn't you!" If you'd waited till morning and hadn't jumped to conclusions, you might have caught everyone in a more rational mood. And perhaps, even more significantly, discovered the facts.

By the way, the facts in this case were: Little sis didn't borrow the jumper. Mum realised you had meant to put it in the wash and so had added it to the washing pile. Unfortunately, she had dropped it on the way to the washing machine. Sis had gone out and her boyfriend had finished with her (probably because of the colour of her jumper). She was upset and everyone else, including the dog, had come out in sympathy. Now who looks stupid?

I think it's time for a more thought-out strategy for confrontations!

1. Pick your battles. You can't spend your life fighting every battle. You'll end up a wreck and let's face it some battles just aren't worth it. In fact, some are positively worth losing! To compromise where possible can increase good will for when you have a battle which is worth fighting and winning! A good relationship with Mum and Dad, brother and sister, may be worth more in the long-term than the fact you have to watch *Emmerdale* rather than *Top Of The Pops*.

You may say they never remember the concessions I make. Well, they may forget, but you needn't. I'll come back to that!

2. Pick your moment. Fighting when everyone is tired or obviously fed up may make for more excitement but the chances of a reasonable settlement are pretty low, don't you think? More likely it will become a fight to the death over something previously no-one could care less about. It may be that you can win concessions out of a preoccupied dad. But if you're only interested in winning the arguments you consider important, I'm afraid you are not destined to become a peacemaker in the family!

3. Remain calm and rational. If you're someone who gets heated very easily or else knows what you think but has trouble putting it into words, this won't be easy. In which case it is even more important you pick your moment correctly! Be sure of what you want. Is it that important? Be sure of your arguments. Are they reasonable?

Most arguments are won not by what is said, but by how it is said. And that has as much to do with calmness and reasonableness as cleverness. If you've thought through your argument carefully, you can point out that you have been prepared to compromise in other situations. If you're calm, you're also much better placed to listen. Getting worked up only tends to get others worked up, making sure that they strengthen their arguments. And in any heated argument with your brother or sister, there is always the likelihood that Mum will rush in like the US cavalry, and with no questions asked, break up the fight. Fights stopped in this way are rarely resolved according to justice!

4. Be ready to apologise. How you respond at the end of an argument is as important as at any time during the argument. For future relations and differences of opinions, it pays to be grateful when getting your way, gracious when not and, most importantly, honest when wrong. Sorry may be one of the hardest words to say, but it is also so powerful. It is easier to like, forgive and respect someone who is prepared to say sorry and mean it. Saying sorry can also be contagious.

5. Pray. Disagreements are never easy. They are particularly hard if you have them with someone, who is often irrational and inconsistent and never, but never, wrong. Well, never as far as he or she can remember anyway. God does understand. Jesus met a few unreasonable people during His time on earth. He was crucified by a whole bunch of them. Try to pray about things before you get drawn into an argument. Pray about your position. Make sure it is as reasonable, important and justifiable as you think it is. Then pray for your family.

Afterwards, you might need to pray that the sun shouldn't now go down on your anger, but that you can forgive and get on with loving and peacemaking. You should pray for your family, for the best for them, whatever the result of the argument.

Being a peacemaker doesn't mean you'll never argue. But it does mean that you should spend more time encouraging than confronting. A lot of arguments needn't happen if there was more encouragement, appreciation and love expressed within the home. Unfortunately, these qualities don't come easily to people. They can, though, be contagious. All it takes is a carrier to get everyone going. That is the job of a peacemaker and that is what Jesus calls you to be.

HONESTY TEST 9

Tick the box at the end of the statement which best describes you.

1. Do you enjoy a good argument or sulk?
   a. Yes. ❏
   b. Sometimes. ❏
   c. Only once in a while. ❏
   d. Never. ❏

2. Do your arguments tend to get more heated than rational?
   a. Most of the time. ❏
   b. Occasionally. ❏
   c. Never. ❏
   d. All the time! ❏

3. In your family arguments is someone prepared to step down?
   a. Most of the time, and usually the same person. ❏
   b. Most of the time, and different people. ❏
   c. Never! ❏
   d. Sometimes. ❏

4. We are prepared to say sorry in our family.
   a. Most of us, most of the time. ❏
   b. None of us at all. ❏
   c. None of us unless pushed! ❏
   d. Some of us, some of the time. ❏

5. I pray for my family and our relationships.
   a. Never or rarely. ❏
   b. Sometimes. ❏
   c. Most days. ❏
   d. Everyday. ❏

(Turn to page 160 if you want to find out how you scored.)

Now get out of that!

Was she imagining it or did this stranger really know? He couldn't do, could he? Surely it didn't still show?

It was the way he looked at her that was unnerving her. You see, she knew about "looks". Only weeks before it had been her job to pinpoint what a man was thinking, and indeed wanting, just from the most casual of glances. Such was the skill of an experienced prostitute, that a potential but nervous client could be instantly recognised and encouraged.

But now she feared those looks which before she would have welcomed. Then they had promised hope for a few weeks' living. Now they were icy reminders of all she had abandoned those few weeks past when she'd met Jesus.

To be honest, she wasn't sure whether the man who today sat by the well resting from his journey really did recognise her for what she had been. Perhaps his quick glance had caught some sense of shame in her eyes, or perhaps she was just imagining it. All she knew was that as she now sought to live for Jesus, she hoped above everything else she could leave her past behind her. All she wanted was to make a fresh start and live for the most amazing man she'd ever met.

Her friends couldn't understand it, that was for sure. "The most amazing man I've ever met". They'd laughed when she'd told them that. It was the sort of laugh she would have enjoyed herself before; coarse, bawdy, full of innuendo. Now it hurt. They'd laughed again when she said she was going to change, and they told her they'd see her the day after next. Again she could understand it. The thought of her being religious was ridiculous! She could understand it, but it still hurt. It hurt that people were so cynical about her. It hurt that none of her friends expected her to last for long. It hurt that they were waiting for her to fail. Her friends! They were a motley crew but they were her friends.

Were her friends? If her old life was truly gone, perhaps her old friends were too. For a moment a cloud came over the sun and she shuddered with the early evening breeze. Then as quickly again, the cloud was gone and as she looked up, she grinned, seeing another man had returned to the well. The man who had changed her whole life. The Son of Man, as He called Himself. He returned her smile. Surely He was the only one in this town who really knew the truth about her. But the look He gave her was very different. It was a look which renewed her confidence that not only was her past behind her, but it was forgotten and its hold on her was broken for ever.

She looked at the figures around her and allowed herself a quiet laugh. So what if they did know her past? Who cares what they may be whispering to one another? Jesus believed in her. To be honest, that was all that mattered. Another shiver went down her back, this time not due to the chill but the excitement. She was free. (27)

Although the story of the sinful woman in Luke chapter seven is not one directly related to family, I decided to tell it because it's easy to relate to how she probably felt. She'd messed up and wanted to change. But my guess is that even though Jesus forgave and accepted her, others were less accepting and much more cynical about how long the change would last.

You may have been at war with one of your family for what seems like ages. You want to stop but don't know how. You may have betrayed your parents' trust and abused alcohol, cigarettes or drugs. They may not know, but you do. You may have got involved sexually in a relationship you know is wrong. Mum may know, she may not. You want to get out of it, but don't know how. Not easily anyway.

Change isn't easy. First there's the humbling involved in admitting mistakes. Then there's the humiliation when people respond to your admission. They may laugh, be cynical or delight in embarrassing you. There could also be hurt involved as you have to admit to things which others you love may be shocked or hurt by.

It may be awkward or difficult afterwards, and all the time you may fear that it won't last or work and you'll mess up again. This last fear may be all the more acute if you know there are people around you just waiting for you to fail, expecting it, looking out for it and delighting to point out any hint of it.

I want to encourage you, though, to face up to your responsibilities, to come clean with God and put right what you know is bringing great pain to Him and damaging your relationship. He will forgive you in the same way He forgave the sinful woman. Then as far as possible, try to be honest and open with Mum and

Dad. Admittedly, I don't know your mum or dad, but I have been encouraged enough by stories I've heard to know that by facing up honestly to failure, families have become closer and offered the kind of support to one another which God can use to free us from the past and set us on our feet for a brand new future. Here are three such stories.

Sally's story

Sally loves her dad very much. They have the sort of relationship in which they can talk about anything together. Well, almost anything. One thing they obviously didn't talk much about was sex, which was a shame because when it came to the crunch, Sally's ignorance cost her dearly.

Sally was never really sure whether she loved Terry. She felt sorry for him and, anyway, he was a boyfriend at a time when everyone else at school had one and she needed one. He was also a bit older than her and had a job. These two facts gave him an extra high rating in her friends' eyes. Incidentally, he was also far more sexually experienced than Sally, but that didn't worry Sally unduly because to be honest: who wasn't more sexually experienced than her? Certainly, the whole sixth form was, if what they claimed was to be believed; and probably Sally's chief failing was that she believed people far too easily.

Consequently, when Terry suggested they slept together and gave her his assurance it was OK for them to do so as Christians, she believed him. The problem was, despite constant reassurances from Terry, she knew in her heart of hearts it wasn't right. God seemed a million miles away and she thought she knew why! Deep down she wanted to talk to her dad about it, but was scared silly at the prospect. First of all, it was embarrassing. Secondly, it would hurt Dad, and thirdly, what was the point in doing so anyway? So she ...

... told him. They were travelling in the car when Sally broke the news. Dad pulled over, put his arm around her and told her he loved her. He then told her he'd have to tell Mum which he did; and Mum was just as comforting. Sally then knew why she had needed to tell Mum and Dad. Somehow it had helped her get over the guilt of the whole episode and amazingly brought her even closer to Mum and Dad.

Sophie's story

Sophie didn't tell her mum about the mess she got herself into. To be honest, Mum and her were at war! Mum, though, found out for herself: by opening Sophie's mail. You see it really is hard to con a loving parent, even though you may feel you are managing pretty well and ever since Sophie got back from her holiday with her Dad, her Mum had been increasingly concerned with the way Sophie had been reacting and also by the flow of letters from the Isle of Wight!

Finally, she opened the letter and found out the truth about Sophie's fling with a lifeguard! When Sophie came home from school, there was what might be called a free and frank exchange of views. Another way of putting it is that there was a humdinger of a fight! What finally resolved the situation, though, was honesty on all sides. Mum told Sophie how she felt about the episode, how worried she'd been and how hurt she was about what had happened. Sophie told Mum how she felt about having her post opened. Both then apologised for what they had done; and once again the net result was that they were closer than before.

Freddy's story

Freddy thought he was going to die. The room was dark and smelt of sick: his sick. He didn't know how many times he'd been sick since he had got home drunk. All he knew was that he was scared and very, very alone. He wished his mum would come in and help him. She was always there to look after him when he was ill and he knew she was in. So why did she leave him like this? He knew Dad was in too, and to be honest, he wouldn't mind if Dad came into the room and gave him what for. It was just being left alone he hated. He was such an idiot.

Freddy's parents left him for most of the next day, too, until finally he emerged to apologise. He told them he wouldn't do it again and he meant it! They told him why they were upset and he understood it! They then grounded him and he accepted it! There wasn't much else he could do or say. However, Freddy's reaction and subsequent keeping of his word has meant that Mum and Dad haven't lost their trust in him.

It will always take time to rebuild after a major failing but honesty, humility, and openness help. Obviously I can't always promise Mum and Dad will be quite as understanding as Sally's parents were, but you may well be surprised! And of course, there is one person's reaction which we can depend on. God's! As Jesus forgave, and accepted the sinful woman in our story, so He does the same with us. He can change us, and more than that strengthen us to face up to the hurts which might be involved in facing up to and admitting our failings!

SECTION 5

When things go wrong

A look at illness and death in the family and a note on abuse.

This is a rather specialist section which won't be of interest to everyone. So you may want to skip it, although you might find it helps you understand a little better what a friend may be going through.

Life but not as you knew it

It was the Ruddy Duck which set him off.

He only knew that that was what the duck was called, because it said so on a small plaque at the bottom of the picture. "Ruddy Duck by Thomas Jeffreys", whoever he was. He remembered being with Dad when he bought it. It was in Bracknell, of all places, and he was only six. Dad was just out of hospital and Chris had decided he was never going to let Dad out of his sight again.

Ever since then the Ruddy Duck had hung on the bathroom wall. In twelve years he'd never come down. The bathroom somehow had never made it onto the decorating rota. He'd been there all day every day for each of those twelve years, most of it unnoticed. Chris sank back in the bath and thought about this for a while.

The Ruddy Duck was there when Dad had died. Chris was sixteen and in the middle of GCSEs. It had been a terrible shock. Mum was supposed to be the ill one, and then Dad had died. He'd bottled his emotions up and felt so incredibly lonely until a friend had taken him to church and he had become a Christian.

The Ruddy Duck was there the day he had come bouncing home to tell Mum of his new faith in Jesus. He thought being a Christian was wonderful and the answer to all their problems. Mum thought he'd gone monster raving loony.

The Ruddy Duck was there that awful day eighteen months later when Mum died. Chris was in the middle of his A levels. Not that this fact mattered at the time. To be honest, nothing mattered at the time. He just got on, matter of factly, organising the funeral, getting the death certificate, letting out bits of the house and arranging the finances.

Now here Chris was, a few months on, sitting in the bath, fed up with the lodgers who were over the top, happy-clappy Christians, fed up with God for letting him down, fed up with life. He needed to talk to someone. Someone who would understand. Someone who wouldn't smother him with sympathy, but could help him cope with lodgers, God and life. He knew who it would be. He'd known for months. It was just that it had taken months for him to summon up the courage to ring them.

> Chris smiled, sank lower in the bath and nearly drowned. With that he sprang to life. A symbolic spring! Today he sensed he was going to face up to all he'd been bottling up all this time. Today he sensed was going to be the start, just the start, of sorting things out.
>
> "Today might just be significant," Chris said out loud, "And you, you Ruddy Duck, in years to come will be able to say you were there when it happened."

Being a Christian doesn't stop things going wrong. Chris had to learn this lesson just eighteen months after he became one. What being a Christian can do is to help you cope when they do! You may come from a family where you've got used to living on the knife edge of a parent's illness or depression. Or things may suddenly go wrong. One day they are fine and it's business as usual and the next, Dad's collapsed or been involved in an accident. Or Mum's had test results from the hospital that ring alarm bells for everyone. Now in your family there may be life but certainly not as you knew it!

Now I don't want to get you paranoid and leave you scared that at any moment your family could fall apart and die off! But the tragedy is that death is such a taboo subject today that when death or illness does strike, most people don't know how to cope with it. If you're typical, you would have had very little experience of someone close to you dying. This also means that the trauma you would feel if it should happen, would be very hard to deal with.

This section, therefore, deals with death and illness. It covers everything from depression through to long-term illness and finally death. I only have space to think about a parent's illness, but obviously a brother or sister's suffering has a very great impact on the family too, and similar principles will apply. Now the purpose is not to depress you, honest! It hopefully will both explain some of your feelings and also help you cope if your life has been or does get shattered by disaster.

When illness strikes someone you love

1. The pain

Watching someone you love suffer is one of the most miserable experiences. Living with them means you may have no choice but to watch.

Richard was very close to his mum. They'd always had a special relationship, partly because he was the baby and all the others had left home. But when Dad left too, this brought them very, very much closer still. Then Mum became ill with Multiple Sclerosis, a very painful and distressing disease which among other things affects the use of the body.

Richard was shattered by it. Mum was in such pain, often he had no idea how to help. He felt useless. To make matters worse, her pain and frustration often drove Mum to yell at Richard. This hurt him more than anything else. Until in his own frustration, he found himself getting angry back with Mum. In their misery, two people who loved and needed each other were fighting. Because of their love they ended up feeling guilty and even more miserable.

2. The hurts

Richard would often retreat to his room to cry. He'd remember how things used to be. Then he'd feel bitter with God for letting things go wrong and angry with himself for not appreciating Mum properly at the time. As with Chris, little things around the house would set his memory whirling as he thought of how things used to be. Seeing friends with their parents would make him jealous, bitter and angry again.

3. The fears

Sam could get as upset as Richard did. This time though she wasn't crying over the past, but over the future. Like Richard her Dad had left home and when Mum went into hospital for tests, it suddenly hit her she could become an orphan. Her mind went wild at the prospect as she imagined herself being dumped on an uncle she hated.

4. The freak show

Sometimes you've grown up with Mum or Dad's illness. Sometimes a death hits suddenly like a whirlwind which suddenly rips through your life, leaving a trail of wreckage behind. Sometimes illness can hit suddenly and just stay. Finally Mum or Dad's depression may come and go. Like an unwelcome guest you're never sure when it will show up or indeed how long it will stay.

Nearly everyone whose family goes through some form of difficulty or tragedy wonders whether their family will ever be normal again. It can be so hard to get on with life. When Debbie's dad needed a liver transplant, for instance, all the family sat waiting for the phone call telling him to come to hospital straightaway. It was like living in a waiting room for nine months. Or as Debbie described it: "It was like the whole family was pregnant!"

As Debbie found out, getting on with life in these circumstances isn't easy, and this can be both frustrating and embarrassing. Chris's parents seemed to die at just the wrong times, right in the middle of his exams. Not that Chris held it against them! Helen's mum also timed her depression nicely to coincide with any major exam or move Helen made, and in this case it was harder not to be cynical. When Abi's dad was ill it was impossible to bring anyone home. There was need for constant hush about the house and any friends visiting would have felt terribly awkward.

5. The loneliness and grief

When death comes, it may come as something of a relief to all concerned. But it will always be painful. All the feelings of pain, hurt, fear and unreality experienced at the outset of Mum or Dad's illness come back for a repeat performance. Only this time they team up with other feelings like loneliness and loss and together form a massive dose of grief.

It may take a while for everything to sink in. When Abi's dad died, she felt odd. In fact, she felt nothing. Nothing that was until about a year later when everything suddenly hit her. When Chris's mum died soon after Dad, he found himself being businesslike and coping, until all his emotions came out about four months later. At these moments both Abi and Chris wanted the same thing: someone to talk to.

How to cope with the grief

1. Don't bottle up your emotions

You may find it very hard to express your feelings for a number of reasons. Perhaps you come from a family who find it hard to show how they feel. Perhaps you feel you ought to be strong to help the others. Perhaps you don't know who to turn to. To turn to family might just add to their problems and to go outside the family might seem like letting them down. Perhaps you are just scared about breaking down.

It is important though to grieve. Grieving seems to be the way God designed to help us cope, so expressing your feelings of sadness is nothing to be ashamed of or frightened of. In fact Jesus was sad when He saw illness and wept when He saw death.[28] If you don't grieve it may make it harder for the pain to go away.

It is best to find someone to whom you can turn, rather than to get upset on your own. God gave us one another to support each other and you shouldn't feel embarrassed about leaning on someone in a time of need. If you don't, then your pain is more likely to get on top of you. You might get down and feel very, very lonely.

If you do try to cope on your own, you'll find it hard. There'll be times, at home with your family, when you feel very low. Then you might get angry and take it out on those you love. Alternatively you may find yourself keeping out of the way of your family or trying to detach yourself from the problems at home. Either way, the signals you'll be giving are that you don't care when the truth is that, far from not caring enough, you care too much and can't cope. Now you feel misunderstood and guilty.

Chris found a couple at church to talk with. They hadn't pressurised him to do so, but had told him that he could always chat if he wanted to. It took him four months to do so, but then they were able to help him through the difficult times like Christmas, when he was able to join in their celebrations. But what Chris perhaps appreciated most was that they were just there to listen whenever he wanted them.

Try to find someone somewhere whom you feel has the time and understanding to help you. You will probably be surprised just how many folk in your church would love to help.

2. Ask the questions

Like Chris and Richard you might have a lot of questions to ask of God. This is natural. Don't think you need to pretend your faith is so strong it never doubts. For four months Chris put on a show with folk from his church and pretended he was doing fine. He wasn't. He honestly didn't need to pretend, and neither do you.

You may feel you'd like to protect some of your family from your questions and that's fair enough ... so long as you have someone somewhere to turn to. The trouble with unanswered questions is that they don't go away, they just fester beneath the surface. The Bible positively encourages us to be honest with God. Far from burying the subject, a whole book in the Old Testament, Job, is given over to questions about suffering. A number of the Psalms, too, are very, very blunt in their questioning of God.[29]

You've probably not come across Lamentations. It's hidden away just after Jeremiah. Most people don't bother with it because it's about grief and they find it depressing. On the other hand, if you are grieving you may be able to relate really well to its thoughts and questions.

God understands. His love for your family is perfect and, therefore, the pain He feels is just as total. He knows how you feel. He knows how hard it is to pray sometimes and how preoccupied you can become with the problems. You can tell Him exactly how you feel since He is listening to your heart anyway. He hears its ache and cry. He shares it. You can talk to Him.

3. Don't give up on life

It may be very hard to carry on with your life when your home is in turmoil. You may not feel like going out and enjoying yourself or else you may feel guilty about doing so. You may feel you ought really be staying at home looking after Mum.

The problem is if you take on too much and go under yourself, you'll be no help to anyone. Having a break will enable you to cope and be much more help when you are around. Another point to bear in mind is that often it just makes Mum or Dad feel worse if they feel they are being a burden to you. It can be reassuring to them if you are still able to enjoy something of your life. You may have to force yourself sometimes. But you'll need some relief and normality.

Sometimes home trouble comes at exactly the same time as other important times in your life; like exams! This makes for some very hard decisions. Helen faced this when Mum got depressed and taken into hospital during her GCSEs. She had to decide whether to get involved in Mum's problems or try to shut them out and get her GCSEs behind her. It was an awful decision, but in the end she chose to get on with her work. She shut out the problem apart from one visit a week to Mum in hospital. The good news was she got her exams, Mum got better and they remained close to one another. It was very hard at the time, though!

4. Be encouraged

This may sound totally daft. Be encouraged. I'm not suggesting you start whistling "Always look on the bright side of life" in the face of tragedy. All I would say is that, however dark things may look at one particular moment in time, many, many people come through similar troubles to emerge so much stronger. They have a deeper understanding of God, an inner strength to cope with life, a more real perspective on life, and a greater sensitivity to other people's needs. All things considered they emerge incredible people.

It's true others emerge bitter and broken while still others never emerge at all. But that needn't be true of you if you are able to face up to your feelings, your pain and your questions; and find help. In years to come I'd hope you'd be the sort of person others would immediately turn to when tragedy hits them. Hopefully, they'll be able to see in you something special. As David says in Psalm 23, you've been through the valley of the shadow of death, but you've met God and found comfort there. Now people can look at you and see a person whose life speaks of goodness and love. It speaks of hope and the presence of God.

A word about abuse

Just before I finish this difficult section I want to include a note about perhaps one of the most tragic experiences anyone can know in the home: to be sexually abused. I've talked with a few folk who have been through this trauma and, even if I haven't space to say much, I was concerned enough to plead with you about just one thing.

If you have been abused by a family member or indeed any-one, please don't just lock away the truth of what happened. Everyone I'd talked to had done just that. But the feelings wouldn't go away. Some wouldn't talk because they were scared their family would get angry. Others wouldn't talk because they felt Mum or someone wouldn't be able to cope with what she heard. Others wouldn't talk because they feared they would break up the family. Finally, at least one thought no-one would believe him.

All, though, carried the hurt. One girl hates her brother and ten years on still can't cope with his company. For his part, he seems to despise her. One girl carries the memories with her into any rela-tionship with men and will, if she doesn't sort things out, carry them into her marriage as well.

Today there are a number of people you can talk to. It needn't be in the family or among friends or even in the church. A helpline may be a good place to start and there are some phone numbers at the back of the book. They will be able to help you work out what may be the best course of action in your specific situation. Even if it's an anonymous call, do try something.

SECTION 6

And finally ...

A final encouragement from the story of Joseph.

The honesty tests scoring.

Bible references.

Helpful names, addresses and telephone numbers.

Hope on the horizon

This couldn't be true. He must be dreaming! Joseph was still finding it hard to come to terms with all that had happened over the past few weeks.

Here he stood shoulder to shoulder with Simeon, Levi and the rest of his brothers. Never had they been so close as at this moment. Gone was the jealousy, the hatred, the scheming and, he had to admit it, his own self-righteousness. God had done some pretty amazing things. It had taken a lifetime to happen, but here they were, expecting any time now to be a complete family again.

They stood together scouring the horizon, silently expectant. Soon their father would appear as a tiny dot on the distant desert road, and then their family would really be complete again. The treachery, heartache and separation would be a thing of the past. Joseph shuddered again. It was as though his body couldn't cope with the enormity of the occasion and the emotions. His beloved father had suffered so much. With hindsight, Joseph knew that his dad was probably to blame for much of what had happened, even though he was uncertain exactly why Dad had made the mistakes he had. Perhaps it was that ...

His thought processes were interrupted abruptly by the tiniest of disturbances. There, that faint, blurred sand cloud, still miles away, signified the coming of his father and with him the fulfilment of the hopes and dreams of all those wretched years.

The dam of silence broke and the excitement which had been building up over the weeks, days and final hours simultaneously overflowed out of each of the brothers. They strained to see and pick out the details of the slowly approaching entourage. They pointed out familiar figures to Joseph as they recognised them.

There was Dinah. Her brothers had said little about her, which had surprised Joseph. He would have expected something from Simeon and Levi at least. Why hadn't she married? What tragedy had befallen her? What secret pain did she and the family still carry? Joseph guessed it would come out in time, but it wouldn't be now. Now was the time of reconciliation. The brothers, their father and Dinah. The impossible was happening. His broken, embittered family was becoming one again. More one than they'd ever been.

It was beyond even his wildest dreams![30]

Well done for having made it to the end! I hope you now understand your family better and have more idea of how to cope with them. Most of all, I hope I've inspired you to see that there is so much more potential in your family. You may come from a very loving family, but are you able to express your faith and love as much as you'd like? You may come from a very difficult family, but you needn't give up on them. After all, you probably don't come from a family more mixed up than Joseph's, and God could do something in his family, despite all the pain on the way!

I realise that a lot of the advice I've given has involved talking about things. I also realise this may require quite a lot of courage. If Mum, Dad, brother or sister has been particularly hurtful in some way, talking may not only be hard, it may also seem quite pointless. I hope and pray you will be surprised, though. Then again you may think there is no one outside of the family to talk with, however much you wished there was someone. Again though, please don't give up hope too quickly. You may not know who they are to begin with, but I am convinced that God will have someone. The Bible tells us "our God can supply ALL our needs according to His riches in heaven".[31] That really does mean ALL.

Finally, I hope I've inspired you enough that you will now make the most of both your families. Yes, I did mean "both". It may seem a long way off, but in around twenty years time, who knows, a teenager might be sitting down to read a book like this. As he or she reads it, my hope is he or she would be able to turn to you and tell you that you're pretty good ... as mums and dads go!

Honesty test scoring

If you add up your total points on each honesty test this may help you think some more about how the advice given in each section might apply to you and your family. Please, though, don't read overmuch into these honesty tests results. They aren't meant to give expert analysis into your family, but just get you thinking. To be honest, your family like every other is unique and, as such, it is impossible to make simplistic generalisations.

Test one

Q1: a 2, b 3, c 4, d 1.
Q2: a 2, b 3, c 4, d 1.
Q3: a 1, b 2, c 3, d 4.
Q4: a 2, b 3, c 4, d 1.
Q5: a 2, b 3, c 4, d 1.
Q6: a 3, b 4, c 1, d 2.
Q7: a 4, b 1, c 3, d 2.

23–28 You seem to get on very well with Mum and Dad.
17–22 You get on well but perhaps things could be better. Think through the ways you can improve your relationship.
11–16 There seems to be a lot of room for improvement. Carefully work through the seven ways you can make a difference.
7–10 If you're right, you could have *big* problems. But I guess you didn't need me to tell you that!

Test two

Q1: a 4, b 3, c 2, d 1.
Q2: a 3, b 2, c 1, d 4.
Q3: a 2, b 1, c 4, d 3.
Q4: a 1, b 4, c 3, d 2.
Q5: a 4, b 3, c 2, d 1.
Q6: a 3, b 2, c 1, d 4.

19–24 You seem a remarkably balanced family!
14–18 Things seem good but not perfect. Look through the two charters and work out what you could do to make things better.
10–13 Think through the charters very carefully. There must be ways you can improve things.
6–9 Oh dear! Don't give up, though!

Test three

Q1: a 4, b 3, c 2, d 1.
Q2: a 2, b 1, c 4, d 3.
Q3: a 1, b 2, c 4, d 3.
Q4: a 3, b 1, c 2, d 4.
Q5: a 4, b 3, c 2, d 1.

17–20 It is possible to come through the trauma of family breakdown OK. Young people like you prove it.

13–16 In a lot of ways you probably feel OK. But think through those things which do still hurt, and where appropriate find someone to talk to about them.

8–12 You're obviously carrying a number of hurts, but you're not abnormal nor is the situation hopeless. Find someone to talk to.

5–7 You must feel very hurt and to find some healing you will need help. Don't hide your feelings, but find someone to talk to however hard it may appear to be.

Test four

Q1: a 2, b 1, c 4, d 3.
Q2: a 1, b 4, c 3, d 2.
Q3: a 4, b 3, c 2, d 1.
Q4: a 3, b 2, c 1, d 4.
Q5: a 2, b 1, c 4, d 3.
Q6: a 1, b 4, c 3, d 2.
Q7: a 4, b 3, c 2, d 1.

23–28 You're either brilliant or telling porkies.

17–22 Not bad, but think through ways you can make life easier for brother and sister and how you can get closer.

11–16 You've a lot of thinking and working things through ahead of you.

7–10 If you're right, I'm glad I don't live next door to you lot.

Test five

Q1: a 4, b 3, c 2, d 1.
Q2: a 3, b 2, c 1, d 4.
Q3: a 2, b 1, c 4, d 3.
Q4: a 1, b 4, c 3, d 2.
Q5: a 4, b 3, c 2, d 1.

17–20 I hope my kids turn out like you.

13–16 Not bad, but follow through on my advice and see what could make things better.

8–12 You probably feel that you've got some problems. Look particularly at the survival steps which apply to the questions you scored lowest on.

5–7 I think it might be time for some blunt talking. Think about it.

Test six

Q1: a 4, b 3, c 2, d 1.
Q2: a 3, b 2, c 1, d 4.
Q3: a 2, b 1, c 4, d 3.
Q4: a 1, b 4, c 3, d 2.
Q5: a 4, b 3, c 2, d 1.
Q6: a 3, b 2, c 1, d 4.

20–24 Your family and church sound great.

15–19 Not bad, but I'm sure you'll agree it's worth working through some things.

10–14 It sounds as though there could be quite a lot to work through. Do try, though, won't you?
6–9 Have you tried talking about these things? Don't reject everything without first trying every way to sort things out.

Test seven

Q1: a 4, b 3, c 2, d 1.
Q2: a 3, b 2, c 1, d 4.
Q3: a 2, b 1, c 4, d 3.
Q4: a 1, b 4, c 3, d 2, e whatever you scored on Q3.
Q5: a 4, b 3, c 2, d 1.

17–20 They're very tolerant. Keep praying.
13–16 They're probably not too bad really even if they seem difficult at times.
9–12 Tricky. But not impossible: keeping praying and showing the reality of your faith.
5–8 This sounds pretty difficult. Do make sure you find someone to talk with about it.

Test eight

Q1: a 1, b 4, c 3, d 2.
Q2: a 4, b 3, c 2, d 1.
Q3: a 3, b 2, c 1, d 4.
Q4: a 1, b 2, c 3, d 4.
Q5: a 2, b 1, c 4, d 3.
Q6: a 3, b 2, c 1 and 4!

Don't add your score up this time. Just see what you got most of. If you got:
Mostly 3s you're doing very well or to be more precise Mum and Dad are!
Mostly 2s isn't bad but there's obviously some tensions.
Mostly 1s means your parents could be exerting pressure and you need to think through the advice I've just given very carefully.
Mostly 4s probably leaves you quite insecure. You may not find it easy to talk to people. But I'd try. It sounds as though you need someone to show interest.

The big, big honesty test

Q1: a 4, b 3, c 2, d 1.
Q2: a 3, b 2, c 1, d 4.
Q3: a 2, b 1, c 4, d 3.
Q4: a 1, b 4, c 3, d 2.
Q5: a 4, b 3, c 2, d 1.
Q6: a 3, b 2, c 1, d 4.

20–24 I'm really pleased to hear it.
15–19 Not bad, but you obviously have your moments!
10–14 I think you could need to do a little more thinking for yourself.
6–9 I'm not sure there's much I need to say!

Test nine

Q1: a 1, b 2, c 4, d 3.
Q2: a 2, b 3, c 4, d 1.
Q3: a 3, b 4, c 1, d 2.
Q4: a 4, b 1, c 2, d 3.
Q5: a 1, b 2, c 3, d 4.

17–20 If you were a Brownie you would have won your peacemaker badge.
13–16 Not bad most of the time. Think about the "some of the time" though and work out how you can improve.
8–12 It sounds as though you all get a little hot under the collar sometimes! Give this chapter a bit more thought!
5–7 It sounds as though you could need to call in the United Nations Peace Keeping Force.

Bible references

1. 1 Samuel 20
2. Genesis 1:20–31
3. Isaiah 66:13
4. Deuteronomy 1:31
5. Jeremiah 31:3
6. Ephesians 6:1–4
7. Proverbs 13:1
8. Genesis 9:18–27
9. Genesis 25:19–34; 27:1–40
10. Genesis 1:27–28; 2:15; 3:17–19
11. Hosea 1:2–9
12. Genesis 30:19–21; 37:1–11
13. Mark 3:20–35
14. Luke 2:41–52
15. 2 Peter 3:9
16. 1 Peter 2:12; 1 Timothy 4:12
17. Judges 6:11–40
18. Jeremiah 29:11
19. John 10:10
20. Deuteronomy 32:10–12
21. Joshua 1:9
22. Psalm 42:7
23. Luke 9:51–55
24. Matthew 20:20–28
25. Matthew 5:9
26. Ephesians 4:26
27. Luke 7:36–50
28. John 11:32–36
29. e.g. Psalms 60; 73; 74; 143
30. Genesis 45; 46:1–7, 28–34
31. Philippians 4:19

Information and Helplines

To read when your family is splitting up:
How To Stay Sane When Your Family's Cracking Up — Colin Piper, Chris Curtis and Tim Dobson (Scripture Union 1993)

Confidential helplines for young people
(These calls are free)

Child Line: 0800 11 11

NSPCC: 0800 800500